drama

A handbook for primary teachers

Geoff Readman

Gordon Lamont

The authors would like to thank the following for their suggestions and help in trialing drama material: the staff and pupils of Aboyne Lodge Primary School, St Albans; the staff and pupils of Spencer School, St Albans; the drama students at Bishop Grosseteste College, Lincoln; Pam Curtis, primary teacher, Nottinghamshire; Wakefield Drama in Education Team; Humberside TIE. The authors would also like to acknowledge the influence of Jonothan Neelands, University of Warwick, and Nottinghamshire Drama and Dance Support Service.

Published by BBC Educational Publishing,
BBC Education, White City, 201 Wood Lane,
London W12 7TS.

© BBC Education 1994

Designer: Jo Digby
Photographer: Chris Fairclough
Editor: Barry Kruger

Photograph acknowledgements:
Mary Evans Picture Library p. 121; Museum of Childhood, Edinburgh p. 72; National Portrait Gallery, London p. 123.

This book is set in 12/16 pt Janson text

Page make-up by Goodfellow & Egan, Cambridge
Printed by Bell & Bain Ltd

Contents

About the authors

After training at Bishop Grosseteste College, Lincoln, Gordon Lamont taught drama at Frank Wheldon School and Fairham Community College, Nottingham, where he became Head of Drama. He has been part of the Nottingham Playhouse Roundabout Company, spending three years with the Theatre in Education team working mostly in primary schools. During his career at the BBC, he has been Producer of School Radio programmes such as *Drama Workshop*, *Verse Universe*, *Let's Make A Story*, *First Steps In Drama* and *Something To Think About*. He is now working on schools programmes for both radio and television. His books include *Move Yourselves!* and *Drama Toolkit* for the Bible Society, and *Something To Think About*, a collection of poems, songs and stories from the BBC School Radio series.

Geoff Readman is Principal Lecturer in Course Development at Bishop Grosseteste College, Lincoln, with specific responsibility for drama. He began his career teaching drama in a primary school, before becoming Head of Department in a comprehensive school. In 1976 he was appointed Leader of Wakefield Drama in Education Team and Director of Wakefield Youth Theatre. During the 1980s he was Inspector for Drama in Nottinghamshire directing DES and LEA courses in Drama, examining Diploma Courses and advising on GCSE practical course-work for MEG. He has been a visiting tutor for Residential Drama Courses for Teachers in many LEAs, is a reviewer for the Times Educational Supplement and was the first chair of National Drama. His publications include *Drama in the Market Place* (2D Publications), *Participation and Performance in Theatre in Education* (Loughborough University) and *New Partnerships in New Contexts* (1993) in *Learning Through Theatre*.

The primary aim of this book is to support teachers who are new to drama or wish to develop their drama skills

HOW TO USE THIS BOOK

The book is divided into four main sections. You can refer quickly to the sections using the bars printed at the side of each page.

- Section one, which begins on page 7, is entitled What is Drama? This explores the authors' understanding of the role and place of drama in the primary school.

- Section two, beginning on page 43, is a Guide to Drama Forms. This defines the various approaches to drama which are used in the practical sections.

- Section three (pages 72-126) offers practical ideas for use at pre-school level, Key Stage 1 and Key Stage 2 (ages seven to nine and nine to twelve respectively).

- Section four contains further reading lists and resources.

The practical ideas in section three are presented in two forms:

— as plans for a lesson or series of lessons, with detailed suggestions as to how the drama may be developed;

— as *Snapshots* where starting points for exploration are clustered around a central theme and aims.

This is a book to be used by individual teachers or groups of teachers to enhance their practice.

How you use the book will depend on your teaching situation, your experience of drama and your own preferred working method. We suggest some possible approaches below.

If you are just beginning to explore your understanding of the role of drama...

Refer to the What is Drama? section. You may find that there are statements made which you find hard to apply. This should not be a cause for concern since drama is a developmental process in which different teachers and groups of children evolve their own ways of working. We suggest that you continue by reading any of the practical lesson plans which suit the age group which you teach.

Where a particular form of drama is suggested, refer back to the Guide To Drama Forms section, beginning on page 43. This section gives further examples of the types of drama referred to, along with suggestions for how they may be developed.

The really important part of this process is to try something out, see how it works and feed that experience into your next attempt at classroom drama, perhaps using further ideas from this book to help you develop your practice.

When you are ready to develop your own lesson plans...

...refer to the section headed 'A framework for drama' (page 17), and the advice given in the sections on planning, implementation and assessment.

If you feel more confident with drama...

...you may want to go immediately to the practical suggestions, referring back to the reference section as appropriate. We would still advise using the What Is Drama? section, to raise questions about drama and its place in primary education, but you may prefer to do this alongside your use of the practical examples.

What is drama?

Contents

Introduction

Drama has more to offer a school than simply helping children to acquire specific curriculum skills and techniques

Drama is an interactive, living art form which reflects a variety of styles, genres, and approaches. Within a balanced primary curriculum it can involve children in movement, dance, reading texts, adopting role, radio drama, group play-making, mime, acting, and a host of inter-related activities. There are as many ways of teaching drama as there are teachers teaching, and our hope is that the rich diversity which currently exists continues to develop in the future. The ideas in this book are intended to extend knowledge, whilst encouraging teachers to build upon their existing classroom practice.

There are certain guiding principles which inform and underpin all effective educational drama, and these principles have shaped the practice described in this book.

- Drama should offer children safe and secure contexts, within which ideas and concepts can be explored.

- Drama is an art form in its own right, as well as a cross-curricular learning medium.

- Drama is a practical and social art form which draws on the knowledge, interests and enthusiasm of those involved.

- Drama teaching is about extending children's ideas and deepening their understanding of the issues involved.

Drama has more to offer a school than simply helping children to acquire specific curriculum skills or techniques. In those schools where a drama policy exists, with specific aims and clearly defined stages of progression, children's achievements are considerable. A school which provides a genuine drama entitlement will be offering children regular opportunities:

— to experience a variety of dramatic genres and forms;

— to examine and determine their personal attitudes and values in respect of ethical and moral issues, and the nature of right and wrong;

— to extend and develop their understanding of the full range of narrative arts, including written and oral story-telling, and individual and collective story-making;

— to develop a critical awareness of drama as it appears in the media and in popular art forms;

— to celebrate the uniqueness of their school community through performance and presentation;

— to explore historical contexts through drama and to examine the motivations and relationships of the people involved;

— to make decisions and take responsibility for the consequences of those decisions, within the security of the drama.

The distinguishing characteristic of all drama activity is that it involves children adopting role. Children are engaged in drama learning by behaving 'as if ...' they were someone or something other than themselves. This simple shift in perspective enables children to consider the world from a different viewpoint. They have the security to explore reality and to use drama to comment on that reality. This use of role is a natural human facility of which everyone is capable. Adults act out situations, both mentally and physically, in order to understand personal events and circumstances. Role is sometimes used to prepare for important occasions, sometimes to reconstruct a highly enjoyable event, and sometimes to enable one to cope with personal day-to-day interactions both at home and at work. Children also have this implicit understanding of the pleasure and value of role-taking, as is demonstrated in their imaginative play. Drama is concerned with giving artistic form and focus to this natural, inherent ability.

The examples on the following pages illustrate the learning potential and unique characteristics of imaginative play and drama.

Playing to understand reality

In the corner of a nursery school on a Monday morning, two four-year-old children, Rhanjide and Tracey, are playing hospitals. Tracey, in a white coat, is in the role of Doctor, writing notes on a pretend pad. Rhanjide, the patient, is holding his stomach indicating pretend pains.

Doctor (Tracey): Now, you go home and have some rest, before the Easter Holidays.

Rhanjide, for a second or two, is jolted by this reference to Easter. He raises his eyes and looks quizzically at Tracey, he then nods, indicating that he has understood, and goes back into role as the patient with stomach pain, asking;

Patient (Rhanjide): When is the baby due, Doctor?

In this short sequence of imaginative play there are many different kinds of learning taking place, learning which is being facilitated by the ability of these two children to create an imagined context, (the hospital). It is a context which is enabling the children to explore their understanding of social relationships and cultural norms, as well as helping one of them (Rhanjide) to reconstruct recent family circumstances which have proved confusing. In order that the learning be fully realised, an informed perspective of the situation is needed, which the class teacher could bring. Some of the potential learning within this dramatic action is as follows:

— Tracey is a quiet, reticent child and the imagined context is offering her the opportunity to have a high status position (Doctor) which is normally inaccessible to her in the daily activities of the nursery.

— Rhanjide's mother is having a baby and he has attended the Health Centre with her on several occasions recently. He does not fully understand the Doctor's words to his mother, but he is endeavouring to make personal sense of his family circumstances by replaying the situation.

—These are two children who have always wanted to be friends since the day they started nursery but who have both been slightly reluctant to make the first move. The dramatic context of the hospital has created the ideal social conditions for their new friendship to prosper!

— The children are employing specific communication skills in order for the activity to have meaning (developing appropriate language, adopting clear roles, raising questions and using the play space).

This example of imaginative play demonstrates the natural ease with which young children construct and create imagined and fictional contexts, in order to explore reality. By the simple act of adopting the roles of patient and Doctor, Rhanjide and Tracey are able to examine the world from someone else's view, to express their real feelings and attitudes and to engage in social interaction, liberated by the security of the context.

It is important that primary schools make quality provision for imaginative play and that play is recognised as a learning activity which enables all children to make sense of their world and develop their self-esteem. Although drama and imaginative play are both characterised by the adoption of role, they do have distinctive (as well as common) qualities, as the second example illustrates.

Drama to understand reality

The following account of a lesson highlights some of the significant teaching structures and artistic elements of drama.

A class of ten-year-old children has been doing a long project on Ancient Egypt, the focus of which has been the hidden treasures of the Pharoah Tutankhamun. In the school hall, they have worked in small groups constructing their personal interpretations of the inside of the tomb, using felt-tips, paper, card, cloths and PE equipment. The whole hall is covered with various constructions, which reflect the children's view of the tomb.

At one point in the drama, the children are analysing the moment when Howard Carter, the British archaeologist who was largely responsible for the discovery of the treasures, had decided to go into the tomb alone, unbeknown to the rest of his workers and without the formal permission of the Egyptian Government. The children have looked at his authentic diary entries describing how he felt:

4 NOVEMBER 1922

Something out of the ordinary happened. A step cut in the rock had been discovered.

6 NOVEMBER 1922

Cable to Lord Carnarvon in England. 'A magnificent tomb with seals intact.'

'With trembling hands I made a tiny breach in the upper left hand corner... Widening the hole a little I inserted the candle and peered in... At first I could see nothing, the hot air escaping from the chamber causing the candle flame to flicker. Presently details of the room emerged slowly from the mist, strange animals, statues and gold - everywhere the glint of gold'.

The teacher wants the children to consider some of the ethical concerns contained in Carter's action and has structured the drama so that one child is in the role of Howard Carter. She is peeping through a hole at the entrance to the tomb, holding a candle, and the rest of the class are voicing Carter's feelings and thoughts, as he gazes on the golden figures for the first time. The teacher has asked half of the class to represent Carter's uncertainty about entering the sacred tomb (The Doubtful Mind) and the other half to reflect his excitement, knowing that his discovery will undoubtedly bring long-term fame and fortune (The Excited Mind).

The children are familiar with this kind of poetic action and they stand in two groups, either side of the child who is representing Carter at the entrance to the tomb. The children take full responsibility for the drama, their teacher is there to offer support if needed. As Carter's dilemma unfolds, individuals begin to voice the thoughts which they think might have been in Carter's mind:

The Doubtful Mind

Perhaps I should wait for official permission before entering, it is a grave, after all. Should I enter alone, and in secret? Should I tell the others? What will my friends think, if they find out?

The Excited Mind

So much gold... everywhere gold! I must send a telegram to England - at last the world will know the truth. My life's work fulfilled...

In this example, drama is being used to enhance historical skills and concepts. The children are being asked to utilise their knowledge of the topic, whilst at the same time developing new understanding through the drama process.

There are also other teaching issues to be drawn from this moment:

- The teacher has deliberately intervened and structured this drama, in order to give the children's creativity a focus. The intervention helps to make the drama more meaningful for all the participants.

- There is no risk of history being manipulated or retold by this drama (Carter did actually go into the tomb alone and without permission). However, the process is prompting the class to consider some of the motives, rights, responsibilities and relationships within a significant historical event. The teacher is 'holding still' this moment of history for the children to analyse, rather than hurrying through the plot of the story. This facilitates the kind of enquiry and understanding which is most effective through drama.

- Although there is a strong sense of stillness about the drama, the children are actively engaged as both participants and spectators. Both roles come together as this moment is collectively created. There is no question of needing to re-run the drama in order to make it more effective or to check what each individual has contributed.

- It is as important for children to be given opportunities to spectate and reflect upon dramatic action as it is for them to participate. Many drama lessons are weakened by a view that involvement in drama means physical activity. In any lengthy drama sequence, children will operate as both spectators and participants. Sometimes the two roles will be quite distinctive, but on other occasions they will fuse: the child is simultaneously able to critically reflect and participate.

- The teacher is causing the children to utilise their understanding of previous topic work.

- There are many social skills and techniques being activated by the task. In addition to the drama skills, there is a developing sense of trust, discipline and group awareness.

This is also a moment of collective theatre which exists uniquely for these children and for their teacher. Although the drama process is helping the children understand the story of 'Tutankhamun' a little better, it remains an art form in its own right, with its own intrinsic value.

These two examples are intended to illustrate that imaginative play in the nursery and drama in the classroom are integral parts of the same artistic process, and that Rhanjide and Tracey's use of dramatic action has a direct relationship to that which operates in the Tutankhamun example and in more formal theatre contexts. There exists a rich variety of dramatic forms, contexts and structures, which can all be used by teachers to stimulate different kinds of learning. In the Tutankhamun project many elements of drama and theatre combine to create a moment of productive reflection on a specific historical event. It is important that all forms of drama are recognised for their educational contribution and that teachers feel comfortable and at ease in using any of them as befits their purpose.

What skills does a teacher need in drama?

It is the teacher's task to extend and deepen the children's understanding of the dramatic context. By using certain skills and techniques of intervention, she will provide a control and focus which enables the children to experience a shared sense of purpose. Intervention enables teachers to create structures which challenge children, as well as offering them security and support. In this respect, it is essential that children remain aware of the real and fictional dimensions of the drama, in order to avoid any sense of confusion.

The teacher will develop skills concerned with:

+ negotiating and leading discussion;

+ managing the available space and time effectively;

+ selecting and utilising symbols (eg the candle illuminating Tutankhamun's tomb);

+ structuring productive tension;

+ asking challenging questions;

+ creating opportunities for reflection.

These key teaching skills are given different emphases when the teacher uses drama. More detailed guidance on drama practice is provided in Guide to drama forms (page 43). Our aim is to present a variety of ideas and practice which will enable all teachers to develop effective drama by utilising their existing skills and experience. A child's achievement in drama is not dependent on academic ability, gender, confidence or culture, but on the way in which all of these qualities combine to enable children to create meaning with others.

It is the responsibility of the teacher to:
— resist any assumptions about the kind of role(s) children might adopt;
— select content areas which reflect genuine cultural diversity;
— enable children to adopt roles which challenge any stereotypes;
— offer children opportunities to work collaboratively.

Drama genuinely creates equality of opportunity within the primary curriculum.

A framework for drama

The real excitement of drama resides within the actual doing, which is invariably precarious and unpredictable!

The drama process is such that, once the lesson is underway, new learning and teaching issues emerge continually. Consequently, any framework needs to be flexible enough to take account of the individuality of schools and children, enabling teachers to feel they can use it for their own purpose.

This framework comprises three phases:

For the teacher:	For the children (see page 36):
◆ PLANNING	CREATING
◆ IMPLEMENTING	ENGAGING
◆ ASSESSING	REFLECTING

Planning drama

All teachers plan in their own distinctive way, based upon a variety of factors. However, this framework has been devised on the assumption that teachers tend to start planning from a broad curriculum perspective before focusing on specific details.

The following five stages are always significant dimensions of planning for drama.

i) Social context

This is the ethos of the school and the factors which influence that ethos, which are usually implicit in teachers' thinking. It might be termed 'culture'. This popular term in contemporary education aptly reflects the nature of educational drama: it is an art form which is shaped by the values, attitudes, and relationships of the social context within which it is created.

The following is a checklist for teachers to identify the factors which influence and inform their own planning and which contribute to the 'culture' of their drama.

The school

Does your school have a drama policy?

What priority is given to the development of attitudes and relationships?

How is drama perceived within your school? As production? As music and movement? As relaxation?

Is there a policy of whole-school curriculum planning?

Is drama's contribution discussed at staff meetings? What learning styles are valued?

What resources are available?

Is there a hall or any other cleared space available?

The children

Do the children play imaginatively?

What are the children's views of drama?

What are their attitudes to gender and racial issues?

How well can they work together?

What is the boy/girl ratio in particular classes?

The teacher

Where do you feel most comfortable? Classroom? Hall? Informal or formal learning contexts?

How do you define and perceive drama?

How much experience of drama teaching do you have?

What kind of training do you have?

What kinds of learning do you value?

The community

What is the cultural and ethnic mix within your community?

What is the level of parental involvement?

How is the school perceived in your community?

What are the employment patterns within the catchment area?

Do the children have access to community clubs, societies, teams, etc?

Are there safe play spaces in the immediate vicinity of your school?

All these factors influence how children learn and affect their attitudes within any imagined context which the teacher might select.

ii) deciding on some initial and broad-ranging learning opportunities

How can drama enrich the learning my class currently experiences? Some suggestions:

- to reflect on a recent class excursion/visit;

- to extend class story-time through teacher-in-role;

- to use 'Still Pictures' as a stimulus for writing and discussion;

- to use group play-making to consider moral and ethical issues;

- to give sharing times (assemblies etc.) a greater sense of excitement and involvement;

- to create relevant and tangible connections to remote content, such as volcanoes, Ancient Greece and Vikings;

- to help children find personal meaning within the curriculum;

- to offer children dramatic opportunities to make, plan and design;

- to help children to use knowledge and information in meaningful contexts.

Does my class have particular social needs which drama could address? Some initial ideas:

- to examine a bullying issue;

- to understand the impact of negative stereotyping;

- to be able to work collaboratively and sensitively;

- to respect and value the opinions of others;

- to support a whole-school initiative on 'helping our community';

- to encourage a greater sense of responsibility.

What specific skills could drama help my class acquire?
Some suggestions:

- to use language in more varied contexts in order to develop oral fluency;

- to develop a clearer grasp of story structures (beginning, middle, end, etc);

- to make group decisions more effectively and to develop listening skills;

- to use space creatively;

- to develop presentational skills;

- to extend knowledge of form and types of drama.

iii) Identifying the 'dramatic context' and 'learning focus'

Having considered some basic questions, it is now useful to decide upon the most suitable content for the drama. We have divided what we feel are the most common starting points into two distinct categories, 'dramatic context' and 'learning focus'.

Dramatic context

This is the fabric of the drama: it provides location, characters, story and motivation.

— It can be real or fictional.

— It may be prescribed by curriculum requirements.

— It must have absolute clarity in order that the children feel secure about their real or imagined role(s) within it.

— The detailed information must not hinder the quality of the participation by giving the children too many facts to consider.

Learning focus

This is the purpose of the drama. It might relate to particular skills, to social, emotional or intellectual needs or to specific concepts. The learning focus may be achievable in a one-off session or form an integral part of a longer project.

The learning focus might be to:

- give the class the opportunity to make decisions in small-group contexts;

- highlight the need for awareness of audience, in respect of effective verbal communication;

- enable the class to select appropriate images and symbols.

Remember: it is possible to begin planning a lesson using either a dramatic context or a learning focus; they are interchangeable.

iv) Decisions about the drama structure

In setting up a plan of practice, we find it is best to use the three elements of role, dilemma and tension.

In theory:

ROLE

Role is central to drama. To be effective, all roles must have absolute clarity for both teacher and children. For example:

Who am I in this drama context?

Where am I in this drama context?

When is this drama taking place?

A further consideration in planning is to ensure that children are fully aware of the teacher's expectations of them during the drama. If the learning contract has been effectively established, each child will know how they can influence the decisions and actions in the drama.

DILEMMA

In order that the drama can engage the children, it will require a dimension which prompts their curiosity and offers a range of choices. This quality can be defined as the 'dilemma'. The dilemma will create a focus and instil dramatic tension into the drama and, if successful, make the learning focus achievable. Contexts which contain complex dilemmas offer potentially rich learning opportunities.They comprise events and circumstances which:

— arouse and engage one's feelings;

— prompt questioning and the need for further dialogue;

— pose complex problems,

— cannot be resolved by simplistic actions or responses.

TENSION

Productive tension is a vital ingredient of drama. It relates closely to the dilemma, encouraging the children to feel that the drama is important. Tension gives the drama a purpose and makes it enjoyable. It can be structured through a careful use of such concepts as:

- surprise
- waiting
- ritual
- secrecy
- problem-solving
- space
- danger
- celebration
- devil's advocate
- conflict
- story-making
- narration

In practice:

A class of ten- to eleven-year-old children is studying the topic of canals, and the teacher has chosen to focus on the living and working conditions of the boat people, who lived on barges in the 1930s. In 1930 a parliamentary bill was introduced which was intended to make the children on the boats go to school. This would destroy the family business for many families and force them to split up.

ROLE

Who: family members who own a working barge.

Where: on a barge at an evening meal.

When: an evening in 1930, when the family has recently heard about the Bill.

DILEMMA

The parents want their children to be educated and have new opportunities in life, but they cannot manage the work without them.

Do they sell the barge?
Do they buy a cottage?
Do they send the children away?

What can they do?

TENSION

One of the children is desperate to go to school and she has heard about the new bill. She is frightened to speak at the evening meal, even though she has confided in her brothers and sisters.

She listens intently to her mother and father, waiting for her turn to speak.

What should she say?

Is a dilemma always necessary?

It is not intended to suggest that drama teaching must always be characterised by the exploration of deep and serious issues. But even in the most light-hearted farce or situation comedy, the humour is generally stimulated by the dilemmas in which the characters find themselves. In any event, it should be borne in mind that children experience a great sense of joy and satisfaction when asked to deal with major issues which are normally the remit of adults (planning a playground, deciding to leave Earth).

Human dilemmas are central to effective drama practice. One of the distinctive qualities of all forms of dramatic art is that real-life situations are depicted in order to reveal the many layers of meaning which exist within them. This is as true in plays in the theatre as it is in the play in the nursery.

In Shakespeare's play *Hamlet*, the fact that Hamlet does not seize one of a number of opportunities to kill Claudius and 'sweep to his revenge', gives the play its great tension and allows the audience to ponder the dilemmas facing the characters at the court. Theatre is also about the exploration of issues as much as the presentation of them, and dramatic constraints, like Hamlet's indecision, enable the audience to critically reflect.

In this imaginative play example, two children who are playing at hairdressers are finding the experience of talking in role at the hairdressing salon highly satisfying. They prolong the imaginative play with comments like:

'No, it's still not dry yet.'

'Can you try and set it again?'

'I'll just wait a bit longer.'

Drama, like theatre and play, is similarly concerned with slowing down the action in order that the implications of the context can be considered. The teacher's role is not to direct children through a set of pre-planned events but to help them:

— make decisions and propose alternative action;

— explore the motives within the action;

— make a personal response to the action.

In this sense, we find the concept of a dilemma to be effective in planning and a more satisfactory concept for activating drama than 'issue', 'problem', 'focus', 'learning outcome' or even 'attainment target', although each dilemma will comprise some, or even all, of those concepts.

v) Some final questions

About the Class

Are they ready to work together? In pairs? Small groups? Whole groups?

Is the material appropriate for the age, gender and cultural mix?

What is their current attitude to drama?

Is this the best time of day to introduce drama?

About the Teacher

Is my teaching structure clear?

Have I prepared the space and materials?

Do I know how I want to start?

Have I prepared tasks in relation to available time?

Have I prepared myself?

Implementing drama

Some common questions about drama:

'How can I keep control?'
'Where do I teach drama?'
'When do I teach drama'
'Can drama handle sensitive issues?'
'How long?'

The class teacher is the only person who can realistically determine the most appropriate time, for it depends so much on when she feels personally prepared and sufficiently secure. There is no doubt that drama teaching does require a greater degree of teacher involvement than some other learning methods and that the energy and motivation levels of the children need to be taken into account.

The weekly lesson in the hall, timetabled at the same time each week, can promote a sense of discipline and routine for the children, but we would also encourage drama that takes place in the classroom as part of particular curriculum topics.

In drama, children need to apply themselves rigorously and sensitively if they are to have a rewarding experience. It is not recommended for children who are tired or lacking concentration and should not be reduced to the level of a relaxation session.

In the early stages of implementing drama, it might be best to try out some ideas for a small amount of time, with some very specific tasks. For example:

♦ in the classroom, ask the children to devise 'Still Pictures' which illustrate different viewpoints of Columbus' first landing in America. This might provide an effective stimulus for discussion and analysis;

♦ invite a group of older children, from a different class, to create some playtime accidents which they role-play for your class, who then try to find out more detail about the incidents by asking questions of the roles. This will provide an experience of observing drama and of devising appropriate questions;

♦ in the hall, prepare a sequence of drama where the teacher-in-role strategy is used for a few moments only. The children

have been reading *Jim and the Beanstalk* by Raymond Briggs, (Puffin Books) and the teacher asks the children to remain as themselves while she goes into role as the villager who has been watching the extraordinary events up and down the beanstalk. The children are able to ask the villager (teacher) where he has been and what he thinks is going on. Once the children have developed an understanding of the situation, they are asked to (i) go into role themselves as villagers, (ii) move to a selected part of the hall and (iii) imagine that they are at home discussing whether or not Jim needs to be prevented from going back to the giant, for his own safety.

How do I maintain control?

We recognise that this is a major concern for many teachers, and we hope that the following ideas, techniques and suggestions can help to build confidence.

◇ **The Learning Contract**

One of the most significant dimensions of learning through drama stems from a child's ability to 'hold two worlds in their head at the same time': the real and the imagined. So often poor discipline and inappropriate behaviour, both inside and outside the drama, stems from an absence of clarity about the 'real' and the 'imagined' context, as the child engages 'As if…'. It is most important that a learning contract is established between teacher and children from the beginning so that procedures, expectations and responsibilities are made explicit. As part of the 'contract', simple rules will need to be agreed such as:

◆ how the drama can pause, in order for discussion to take place;

◆ how moments of embarrassment and giggling will be dealt with;

◆ how the teacher will respond to children who want to sit out or observe for a time;

◆ how negotiation will feature in any particular lesson.

The following control strategies deal with some of these issues in more detail.

◇ **Establishing starting-stopping signals**

It is important that the children are clear about how the drama can be paused and how it can be re-started. There will be many occasions when the teacher will want to reflect on what has happened, to raise questions with the children about their motives and actions, or to consider the new dilemmas which have arisen in the drama. There will also be times when the children's behaviour leaves something to be desired and the teacher will want to stop the drama to talk to the whole class.

— Have a physical signal which everyone recognises and which means that the drama has to come to a halt, such as the teacher standing with one hand raised, or making a sound with a tambourine.

— A 'gathering-around' chair at the side of the drama space can also be used by the teacher when it is time for a planning discussion to take place. A useful rule here is that as soon as the teacher sits down, all the class gather around the chair, knowing they are going to talk out of role about their drama.

— Have appropriate clothing available such as a coat, scarf, cloak or headband which can then be taken off to show the children that the drama has paused, only putting it back on when the drama is to re-start.

Different techniques will vary in effectiveness with different classes and there are many other possibilities. Never hesitate to stop the drama on the basis that it will disturb the children's involvement or stifle their creativity. The clearer they are, then the more involved and creative they will be.

◇ **Managing the available space**

The establishment of the working space will enable children to recognise the contribution their imagination can make to the drama. If for example the drama is to take place in an empty space, then they know immediately that most things have to be imagined.

This is particularly important for children at Key Stage One. By establishing the space where the drama will take place, the children quickly recognise what is possible and what the teacher's expectations are. Confusion can often arise in classroom-based drama with Year One children who often refer to actual desks, books and trays, even though the imagined context might be a South American forest or unexplored planet.

Some ideas for marking the space:

◆ in a classroom, a circle of chairs can create the empty space to which the drama will be restricted. The chairs also provide an easy mechanism for holding discussion and 'making plans';

◆ a special carpet, canvas or other material can also create the drama space, as well as being a useful resource in other ways, such as visual displays, play-spaces, etc. Large pieces of material can also be invaluable when the teacher has an imposing hall space but wants to create a sense of informality. They can also be used to mark different locations within the drama.

◆ a thick, large rope is a very simple way in which the perimeter of the drama space can be marked out and defined;

◆ in hall-based work, children often find it difficult to maintain their belief and concentration in certain aspects of the drama, such as the location of a bonfire, a Chieftain's throne, or a river. In these circumstances, the use of conventional PE apparatus can be helpful in building commitment to the fictional situation. However, it is often best to restrict the amount of equipment they are able to use at any one time, otherwise the lesson can easily be concerned with how much equipment the children can successfully remove from the PE store!

It is always important that careful thought be given to the space. This conveys the degree of importance the teacher attaches to the lesson. It may occasionally be more appropriate for the children to prepare the space themselves and decide where the drama will operate.

◇ **Using objects as symbols**

Sometimes children who have behavioural difficulties also find concentration and commitment in drama hard. This can be accentuated by teachers asking them to 'imagine everything!', whereas what is often needed is an effective visual image or object to focus on. For example:

— in historical contexts, secret messages written on old parchment, antique bottles, or census records can enrich the context being explored and provide information for the drama to develop;

— in more recent historical contexts, letters from evacuee children, gas masks, radio recordings or newspapers can give the drama greater authenticity than discussion. BBC Schools Radio drama programmes can provide a stimulating focus in this respect;

— artefacts, prepared by the teacher, can lead to dramas of mystery, secrecy and suspense. For example:

◆ a half written letter from someone requesting help in order to escape from a tyrant or dictator;

◆ a broken toy which is the only evidence of a runaway child's identity;

◆ a St Christopher which everyone who crosses the dangerous cavern has to wear.

The use of objects as symbols in the drama can bind the disruptive class together, can present the embarrassed class with a focus away from their embarrassment, and stimulate the exploration of deeper meanings and implications.

◇ Establishing clear group tasks

One of the most confusing things for children (or adults) is to be asked to get into groups 'to make up a play'. It is important to focus and structure group tasks in ways which make them achievable. It is easier for children to focus if they have only one or two things to think about within the task. For instance:

◆ in a drama about the dangers of Bonfire Night, ask groups to make a still picture called 'The Firework Accident', showing who is responsible for the accident;

◆ in a drama about family pets ask groups to show different ways in which different pets can be encouraged to be part of the family, with minimal dialogue;

◆ in a drama about the market-place, give each group one item of PE equipment to represent their stall and ask them to create a mime showing the stall being prepared at the beginning of the day.

◇ The use and value of other media

Moments often occur in drama when the continuation of dramatic activity might confuse or take the action on rather too quickly. Where it is feasible, writing, drawing or painting can prove a most effective means of analysing the events and actions of the drama. These activities enable direct links between drama and other curricular activities to take place.

For instance:

- children write individual diary entries which are handed in to the teacher at the end of the lesson;

- the whole class draws a collective set of images from the drama, like the Bayeux Tapestry. This could be a simple task, such as 'draw the moments in the drama which you enjoyed today', or a more complex task such as 'design a tapestry which shows the Roman invasion of Britain from the Britons' view';

- individually, children write to a character in the drama, perhaps in the role of the person they portrayed, or as themselves;

- small groups draw road plans of how the new by-pass will affect the village recreation ground;

- the whole class writes out the weekly shopping list for a house-bound senior citizen they have been helping in the drama.

In summary

Once the children have an implicit understanding of the drama process they should be able to make significant contributions to the negotiation of the lesson's focus and to the way the drama should proceed.

All of the control strategies described above are integrally linked to the establishment of the learning contract. There is no doubt that the strategies will:

- provide teachers with the security to experiment and explore new methodology;

- enable children to influence the shape of the drama;

- create time for children and teachers to reflect and analyse the issues of the drama;

- ensure that the drama has a clarity of context, purpose and procedure;

- reduce the risk of confusion about the definition of imagined and real experience.

These suggestions will not necessarily help every child to become involved in drama and it is likely that teachers will need to devise their own particular strategies for dealing with disruption. Sometimes children will respond well to encouraging smiles and humour, and sometimes to direction characterised by frowns and specific instruction.

Drama is such a collaborative learning process that the reluctant learner is more visible, but difficulties experienced by children are not reasons for avoiding drama, they are the very reason for employing it.

Where do I teach drama?

The class teacher is in the best position to decide this. However, the nature of the drama which is possible in a hall is different to the drama that can take place in a classroom. Children will always respond in some way to empty space and a large hall can encourage energetic movement or, alternatively, can make some children feel intimidated.

We appreciate that it is not always possible to be flexible about the use of the hall, but the choice of space is always a significant influence on the drama and should receive full consideration in planning.

Can drama handle sensitive issues?

It is indicative of today's society that many teachers are anxious about using material which might be stressful for some children, particularly if it features some of the emotional problems with which children are in direct contact. This does not only apply to drama. However, drama's strength is that it engages real feelings and emotions in safe, protected and, importantly, fictional contexts.

There will be occasions when teachers will decide against using particular material because it risks disturbing individual children. However, stories, poetry, music, games, teacher's questions, the composition of groups, pictures in books, can all unlock deep emotions for children, unknown to the teacher.

How beneficial are warm-up games?

There are teachers who believe that warm-ups are essential to begin any drama and that warm-ups such as 'tag', 'musical statues' and 'wink-murder' are intrinsic. The playing of non-competitive games can foster a climate of trust, mutual respect and high-quality participation. There are many drama-orientated games which will create a classroom atmosphere of shared excitement for both teacher and children alike. However, game-playing may not be the most appropriate way to begin a drama session, and games may not always create the right frame of mind for children to enter a drama. In our experience, the benefits of playing games need to be carefully considered within the chosen learning context.

In spite of this, there are many positive reasons for using games and introductory exercises. For example:

— physical games can provide an energy release at an appropriate time;

— social games can develop positive interaction and a sense of personal value;

— carefully selected games can introduce the concepts of the drama (eg hiding, the responsibility of sharing secrets, the nature of danger);

—rhythm games can enable the whole group to work together easily.

Thus, games often enable a class to have fun and experience a sense of achievement quickly, as well as helping children to involve themselves in activities such as mime, speech, shape-building, etc.

Games also have their disadvantages and drawbacks:

— they can create an expectation that the drama will be physical and energetic;

— they can make it difficult for children to work reflectively when the drama is eventually introduced;

— they can introduce irrelevant content;

— they can take up valuable time, from which the drama might benefit.

There is a strong case for game-playing being a valuable curriculum activity in its own right, rather than being integrally connected with drama sessions. This is particularly evident when one considers the wonderful atmosphere created through action songs and rhymes in most nursery and infant classrooms.

For more ideas on game playing, see Appendix A (page 127) and bibliography (page 133).

How can I link curriculum drama with assembly and other school performances?

Production and performance have often been the subjects of much debate amongst primary teachers. For some, performance is the goal of drama. To others, drama as a learning process is distorted by any attempt to perform.

Our starting point is that drama in education should begin with the needs of the child and that thinking solely about performance would mean starting with the needs of the audience. However, we do value the role of drama in presenting ideas and in developing curriculum themes into material for assemblies, or for sharing with parents. The lunchtime activities or after-school drama clubs, which provide fun and engagement through performance, are an important aspect of school life, but are beyond our present remit, which is drama within the curriculum.

We also recognise the value that can be gained from showing work to other classes and recognise both the stresses and the reward of developing a production. The word 'developing' is very important here. A poem or picture can be put on display, a computer database can be demonstrated, all without significantly increasing the extra work required or in changing the nature of the original. Drama is different because of its 'live', ephemeral nature. Given this difficulty, it is not surprising that some teachers choose not to use drama for performance, or prefer to have children learn a simple script. There are many drama activities which can be refocused and rehearsed to provide a productive time of shared celebration and we suggest a possible outline for this on page 93: Tricks and Tricksters. There are certain principles which inform performance work:

— the work should be part of the children's own learning;

— children should understand the different dimension that presentation is giving their drama. They should be aware, for example, that when they create a Still Picture, the teacher or other class members might suggest changes for the benefit of an audience. This can be used as a learning focus, by asking groups to step out of the picture one by one to view the whole, as the audience will see it;

— they should be aware of the mechanics of the performance: 'this time, when you do that movement, can you make sure that you all face this way at the end, so that mums and dads will be able to see clearly';

— the teacher should maintain a careful balance between spontaneity and rehearsal;

— the teacher should be prepared to give clear signals so that the children have the security of knowing when to move to the next part of the performance:
'When I read the words - "One day in the forest" - that's your signal to make your forest sounds';

— the nature of any performance should take account of a broad ability range, giving opportunity for all children to participate;

— performance can provide an enjoyable and rewarding experience, but should be built on regular drama inputs where the focus is on learning and sharing within the curriculum.

Assessing drama

Assessment in drama has often proved to be difficult , with teachers resorting to the assessment of theatre skills, rather than the holistic nature of the learning they believe is important. The absence of any national guidance on drama assessment means that schools are able to experiment with different assessment processes and use strategies which are of direct benefit to their own needs.

We are suggesting that drama is made up of three activities for children:
- the ability to create drama
- the ability to engage in drama
- the ability to reflect on drama

Before embarking on assessment, there are two essential questions to be answered:

What precisely is the nature of the learning we are aiming for in drama?

How do we assess it?

What is the nature of the learning in drama?

We have defined the learning into four categories: drama skills and theatre craft, knowledge of dramatic context, group social skills and subsequent learning.

Long-term objectives

- develop new perspectives
- challenge stereotypes
- experience the consequences of decisions taken in drama
- develop independence and clarity of personal ideas
- develop responsibility for personal learning
- clarify responses to ethical and moral issues through drama.

i) Drama skills and theatre craft

* create and interpret stories
* use and understand drama forms to shape material
* use oral and written language in a range of contexts
* evaluate individual and group contributions
* use symbol in various dramatic contexts
* develop a critical vocabulary for drama in all its forms
* communicate through presentation.

ii) Knowledge of dramatic context

* understand and remember facts, actions and motives
* understand other people's living and working conditions
* develop an understanding of how social context shapes events, both real and fictional.

iii) Group social skills

* work effectively in a group
* develop social confidence
* take responsibility
* adopt roles which go beyond the child's self
* develop sensitivity and listening skills
* enhance personal self-esteem
* understand different points of view.

iv) Subsequent learning

* enrich cross-curricular work
* develop a sense of enquiry.

The strength of drama as a learning medium is that elements of all categories are achievable at the same time, all making a specific contribution to the long-term objectives.

It is likely that most teachers would want their classes to experience this central, holistic learning, but if you teach a class which has great difficulty in listening to each other, then the development of their social skills will be the main priority.

How do we assess drama?

Evidence of learning in drama can be collected in a variety of exciting ways, which can almost become as rewarding as the drama itself.

Such strategies might include:

— drawings, individual and whole-class

— writing in role

— actual photographs of key moments; children's own self-evaluation through Still Pictures or verbal accounts

— presentation

— audio-tapes

— video tapes

— diary-keeping

The framework we are suggesting has also been devised with a recognition that assessment will need to be manageable and economic of time.

Opposite is a sample Primary Drama Record (you will find a blank version for photocopying in Appendix B). If you decide to make use of it as it stands, we would make the following suggestions:

1. Only assess four or five children in any single session.

2. Use the 1 - 5 scale as a quick response tick list, extend it if you wish.

3. Be realistic about the number of times individual children will actually be assessed (once a term?).

4. The teacher's and children's comments will be the most important dimension of the process.

For convenience, we have restricted the 'Record' to two key skills in relation to each of the three essential activities. The following more detailed objectives are offered as guidance and there are several books listed in Appendix E which present more complex assessment frameworks.

PRIMARY DRAMA RECORD

NAME Rashanara Begum

AGE 8

YEAR 4

	HIGH			LOW		
	1	2	3	4	5	EVIDENCE
THE ABILITY TO CREATE DRAMA		✓				Although Rashanara was very quiet when her ideas were initially adopted, she was highly creative in planning how the volcano could be represented.
◆ TO WORK AND PLAN WITH OTHERS;			✓			
◆ TO ORGANISE AND SHAPE MATERIAL.	✓					
THE ABILITY TO ENGAGE IN DRAMA						Rashanara produced drama which had integrity and sensitivity. Her use of language as the village leader was effective and totally focused.
◆ TO USE APPROPRIATE DRAMA OR THEATRE SKILLS;		✓				
◆ TO PARTICIPATE IN DIFFERENT DRAMA CONTEXTS.		✓				
THE ABILITY TO REFLECT ON DRAMA						As soon as the drama paused, Rashanara did not listen, or concentrate, in our discussions.
◆ TO RECOGNISE QUALITIES IN THE DRAMA AND POSE ALTERNATIVES;				✓		
◆ TO EVALUATE PERSONAL CONTRIBUTION TO THE GROUP.				✓		

CONTEXT OF LESSON

A whole-class drama on a community who live in the shadow of a volcano. They need to decide whether to stay or to move elsewhere.

By the end of Key Stage 1, children should have experienced and be capable of achieving:

The ability to create drama:

- participate in small and whole group discussions

- negotiate decisions about the focus of the drama with others

- listen and respond to the ideas of others

- make suggestions about how to present ideas in drama

- interpret stimulus material

The ability to engage in drama:

- understand and enjoy the relationship between pretence and reality

- adopt role appropriate to the selected context

- speak in role in small and whole group contexts

- use space, sound and movement

- accept the teacher's use of role

- begin to recognise drama forms

- recognise the equal importance of both spectating and participating in drama

The ability to reflect on drama:

- recall and describe the events of the drama

- recognise the key moments of the drama on a personal level

- make suggestions about how the drama might develop

- suggest which drama forms might be appropriate for future development

By the end of Key Stage 2, children should have experienced and be capable of achieving:

The ability to create drama:

- identify and define some of the key drama forms

- negotiate, agree, and implement the focus of the drama, in small and whole group contexts

- respect and tolerate the ideas and opinions of others

The ability to engage in drama:

- recognise the significance of motives and relationships in role-taking contexts.

- adopt role in small and whole group contexts.

- recognise the skills of using sound and movement effectively.

- utilise materials, artefacts, images and objects.

- interpret and create a response to stimulus material.

- shape and devise drama which communicates meaning to others.

- participate in a variety of dramatic contexts.

The ability to reflect on drama:

- reflect on the nature of the meaning created in the drama.

- discuss the effectiveness of the ideas used.

- recognise performance qualities in others and begin to describe particular genres.

- pose alternatives, in terms of ideas, drama forms, or courses of action.

Drama and language development

In dramatic situations, children quickly become aware of the need for a range of language styles, which are shaped by a sense of 'audience' and 'purpose'. Drama is a key strategy for developing oracy skills, as the dilemmas and problems encountered in drama cause children to think and respond with spontaneity. Children often discover they already possess language competencies, as the process facilitates linguistic discovery and growth.

The following chart attempts to present some of the possibilities in simplified form, classifying drama into three key activities, creating, engaging and reflecting:

creating drama

- negotiating what roles to adopt
- speculating on what might happen 'if'
- debating how to present an idea effectively
- explaining personal viewpoints to the rest of the group
- recalling and communicating previous experience
- persuading others of the validity of an idea.

Drama as a context for language

reflecting on drama

- discussing the people and relationships presented in the drama - commenting on the feelings of the scene
- summarising what meaning the drama had
- using effective critical vocabulary
- presenting new ideas and alternatives orally
- predicting what would happen if changes were made to the form or content.
- listing and categorising key issues.

engaging in drama

relating to mood
- formal, in a courtroom drama
- poetic, in a drama on legends or myths
- informal, in a drama about a family birthday celebration
- ritualistic, in a drama about religion or ceremony

relating to role
- appropriate to occupation, such as reporters, time-travellers, conservationists, scientists etc
- appropriate to the lifestyle and social context, such as Victorian children, conspirators, medieval villagers and monarchs

relating to the dilemma
- seeking information by questioning the roles who 'know'
- challenging unfair actions or attitudes
- communicating with other cultures
- explorative and supportive language to help someone who is in a plight

relating to tasks in the drama
- telephone messages and instructions
- interview situations
- giving orders and instructions
- discussing a problem
- listing and categorising key issues.

Guide to drama forms

Approaches to drama are continually developing as teachers apply their own teaching styles to drama forms and ideas.

This section outlines the major strategies and approaches to drama that are suggested in the practical examples beginning on page 72. The list is far from exhaustive: approaches to drama are developing continuously as teachers apply their own teaching styles to drama forms and ideas.

You can use the section on its own to gain a sense of the range of drama forms, or use it in conjunction with the practical sections to add depth to the examples given.

Still Pictures

These are also known as frozen pictures, tableaux, still or frozen images. This strategy involves working in groups, adopting and holding a pose, having agreed its form and structure with the rest of the group.

Its strength lies in its simplicity and in that it requires children to work together in order to explore an idea or situation and then to physically represent it. This helps children to focus on what they think and feel about the circumstances and implications of the drama. It is often used as an initial activity to move from discussion into more active work.

It offers clear and achievable tasks which children often find very satisfying. For example:

- The group will need to talk together, pooling their knowledge of the theme.

- They will need to negotiate the nature of the picture and what it represents.

- They will move from considering these matters generally to choosing and dealing with a specific instance.

- They will work together creatively, each responsible for their own 'shape' within the picture, but with a sense of the whole.

- They will do all of the above within a time constraint set by the teacher which helps to create focus and energy.

Teaching Points

Be specific about the focus and aim of the work.

Encourage groups to talk and plan first - making sure everyone is agreed on what they are doing.

Set a time limit and remind the groups of this as they work - a lot can be achieved in just five minutes.

As the groups work, encourage them to think of the overall shape of their picture. Is it clear what it represents? Is it interesting to look at?

Does it have a variety of postures, different heights - a good use of space?

Still Pictures provide a flexible and accessible starting point and can be used as an initial activity, as a brainstorming process, to explore key moments in a drama, to focus on abstract concepts or as part of other drama strategies. Examples of each of these uses are given below.

As an initial activity

The strategy can be used to get the whole class working together with children responding individually or in groups to key words and phrases such as 'playground', 'our town', 'carnival', 'fireworks', 'television', etc. Each child offers their own Still Picture as an immediate response alongside the rest of the class.

When used for this purpose, Still Pictures also:

— provide a fun start to a session

— form a clear break from what has gone before

— enable the teacher to gauge the mood and energy level of the group.

KS1

Work on Still Pictures of:

- The Chinese New Year celebrations

- Dragons (good fun in a small group situation and requiring organisational skills)

- The seaside (perhaps with the task of presenting many different seaside activities in one picture)

- Giants (can children represent the size of the giant by showing other things/people in the same picture?)

KS2

- Different views of creation (Genesis, Aboriginal 'dream time' etc) to develop drama out of RE

- Olympic games (how can you show movement and action in a Still Picture?)

- Scenes from history (the rest of the class have to guess what is happening and when)

As a brainstorm

The focus of the task provides a motor for the generation of ideas.

KS1

'What animals might you see in a zoo?
Make a Still Picture showing some of the animals'.

or

KS2

'Can you make a Still Picture showing different things that happen in Autumn?'

Having undertaken some written work on the Romans, one might ask the children to depict aspects of Roman life in Still Pictures. This can be a useful spur to recall. The work can be extended by asking the children to make three pictures in quick succession, each showing a different aspect of Roman life.

As key moments in drama

Use Still Pictures to 'freeze' moments of impact, decision, dilemma and emotion.

KS1

'Our spacecraft has crashed, can you show the moment when we hit the moon?'
'Let's create the moment when we first realise that the dragon is crying.'

KS2

'The Native Britons have their first sight of an advancing Roman legion. Make a picture showing that moment. Let your picture give some idea of what the Britons are thinking and feeling.'

'Depict the moment of surrender to a Roman commander. Can the rest of the class tell who are the victors and who are the vanquished just by looking at the picture?'

To explore abstract concepts

Use Still Pictures to draw together themes from the drama, or to connect children's ideas to a central theme.

KS1

Talk about dangerous places - a river bank, a cave, a busy road. Then ask the children to show a dangerous place in a Still Picture which can be developed by combining all the pictures to create a whole class picture exploring the concept of 'danger'.

KS2

Taking the word 'Battle' as the title of the picture, encourage the class to represent the many facets of a battle including, for example:

◆ a family which has been left behind;

◆ the aftermath of a bloody fight;

◆ prayers and supplications for victory.

In a group of five or six, set the challenge of each group member depicting a different aspect of the theme.

Development

Still pictures can be used as the starting point for a wide range of further work.

Use them to pose questions and raise issues:

'Why did Boudica surrender - could she have fought on and won?'

'What does the family think now about the reasons for going to war?'

'Are there occasions when war is the only answer?'

'Why might a cave be a dangerous place?'

'What happens now we have crashed on the moon?'

Then go on to explore these questions through other drama forms. There are particular forms which offer a logical development from Still Pictures: **Living pictures** (page 49).
Speaking thoughts (page 54).
Sound pictures (page 59).

The following will quickly deepen the children's understanding of the meaning of their picture:

Modelling the image

Invite someone from the class to physically move the people in the image to demonstrate how things could change. For example: 'How does the meaning change if we raise the Briton's arm in a defiant gesture?'.

'What difference does this make to how the people in the picture are feeling?'

An effective way of regularly utilising modelling is to:

> i) Create Still Pictures of the key events in the drama thus far.

Then: ii) Ask groups of children to re-model the picture into how they would like the key events to be changed, improved or replaced.

Creating dialogue

'What would the family members be saying to each other as they watch Jim go off to war?' Bring the picture to life or use small group play making to find out.

Hot seating

Bring one role out of the picture and let her be questioned by the rest of the class, who pose questions as themselves, for example: 'What did you see in the cave...Why were you turning away? Why did you look so frightened?'

Living pictures

At its simplest, this means Still Pictures brought to life - pictures that move. Still Pictures can give form and focus, Living Pictures can add detail, depth, new information, and an emphasis on interaction and relationships.

As in Still Pictures, children will need to:

- work together creatively, each with responsibility for their own movement and for the 'look' of the whole.

In addition they will:

- employ their thoughts, feelings and physical movements in imagining themselves to be in someone else's shoes;

- have a different opportunity to portray a situation, idea or feeling by extending the picture through movement.

Examples

KS1

The children have created Still Pictures of the discovery of the dragon's footprints. Ask them to bring the pictures to life showing how they would follow the footprints, keeping eyes and ears alert for any signs of the dragon.

KS2

You are doing some work on Second World War evacuees and you want the children to contrast their lives as city dwellers with their new lives in the country. They have already worked on Still Pictures showing significant daily events in each of the two locations. Now movement can be added to one or two pictures to explore feelings of tiredness, homesickness, elation or whatever.

Teaching points

It is often best to bring the picture to life for only a short time and then freeze the action again, perhaps using this as the starting point for Speaking Thoughts, or pausing the drama to reflect out of role. Good questions are: 'What do we now know about this situation?', 'Does anyone have a problem in this scene?'

Keep a clear focus on the aim of the drama - what is it that you want children to focus on or have some experience of? Build this into the initial setting up of the Living Pictures, and don't be afraid to stop the pictures to re-focus them if the children appear to have missed the point:

'Did the workers look tired in that scene? Was there anything that told you it was the end of a long hard day? How could we change it so that it gives us a better idea of what's been happening?'

Development

Ask the class to think about the sound that could accompany the pictures. Working in silence can be focused and effective, but this is not the only option. You could consider:

- using taped sound effects as in the School Radio drama programmes (see page 135);

- asking the children to create a soundtrack to accompany the Living Pictures (See Sound Pictures below);

- using a percussion instrument to give tension and shape to the pictures;

- combining the pictures with Speaking Thoughts (see below).

Teacher-in-role

Our definition includes all the various occasions when the teacher 'steps into someone else's shoes', either momentarily or for an extended period, with or without the children adopting a role.

The great strength of Teacher-in-role is that by entering the world of the drama with the class, the teacher is demonstrating her commitment to the drama, encouraging the children to believe in the context and to treat the issues with integrity.

A common misconception is that Teacher-in-role has to do with acting, and with taking on a character to give a performance. This is fine, but you don't necessarily have to do any of these things to adopt a role.

At its simplest, Teacher-in-role embodies the same essential quality as children-in-role (though it may be used for different purposes). That is, seeing and expressing something from someone else's point of view.

It is a powerful way of challenging, informing and encouraging the children's own ideas.

Examples

KS1

You are at the point in the drama where the class must decide whether to allow the dragon to visit your school. First, talk together about the kind of questions that the class will need to ask the dragon:

> 'Will you set fire to the classroom?'

> 'Will you trample all over the flowers?'

> 'Will you make too much noise?'

and so on.

Then explain that you will answer for the dragon. When you sit on your dragon seat (a chair that you place for that purpose), anyone can ask the dragon any question which will help you all to decide whether or not to invite him to your school.

Take your seat and encourage the first question - you don't have to abandon your normal teacher role of pointing at someone with a raised hand or encouraging them verbally. You might say something like: 'I really do want to visit your school, why can't I come? What are you worried about?'

Then let the children ask their questions, whilst you respond from the dragon's point of view.

KS2

Adopt the role of a monk at the time of the dissolution of the monasteries. The soldiers are approaching and you must decide what to do: flee? ...fight? ...hide?

The class are in role as villagers who have come to a secret meeting with the monk, they know that they will be punished if it is discovered that they have helped.

Explain your desperate situation and then ask them: 'What should I do?'

Teaching points

Keep your aim in mind and work towards it by your responses and questions.

For instance, in the KS 1 example, perhaps your aim is to help the class value making a decision together, in which case you might ask: 'Well, is there anyone who doesn't want me to come to your school?' or, 'I really do want to come, but I have to fly off and check on my cave soon, so please make up your minds quickly.' At this point you may drop the role momentarily to help the class reach a decision before returning to Teacher-in-role for the class to give the dragon their decision.

Never be afraid to adopt a 'weak' role, one which gives the children greater responsibility. Do not worry about the risk of losing control: this reaction is based on a misunderstanding of the process. You are not becoming the homeless person seeking shelter, you are merely speaking from that person's point of view in order to clarify and move the drama forward. At any point, you have the option of stopping the drama and moving out of role for reasons of control or clarity.

Development

Make use of symbols to help establish when you are in role, and to support the nature of the role:

- a shawl or overcoat to support your role as someone from the cold seeking shelter;

- a headband to represent an agricultural worker in Mexico;

- a bag for migrant workers to carry all their belongings;

- a gas mask for the evacuee.

Combine Teacher-in-role with Speaking Thoughts (see below). The class could ask an evacuee to share her private thoughts as she spends her first night away from home.

Or combine movement with Teacher-in-role as an initial focus. 'I'm going to stand by the door and as I start to move I want you to think about who I might be, and why I'm here'.

You then walk in, as if cold, angry, frightened, injured or whatever provides the right initial stimulus for your theme.

Some Teacher-in-role examples from the practical outlines

High status and authority role: Mompesson in the Eyam project (page 126)

Opposition role: a villager who tells the village about their misuse of the mountain in Giant (page 107)

Messenger role: Minik's friend, Chester Beecroft (page 99)

Low status: - Bruin the bear (page 72)
                 - the child in Dangerous Places (page 92)

Speaking thoughts

This is often used within another strategy (Still Pictures, movement, enactment, for example) and provides an opportunity for class members to speak out loud the thoughts of their role (or others') at any given point.

Examples

KS1

The teacher uses narration to establish the context of the drama:

'The river people have heard the smoking mountain begin to rumble. As they work, the villagers think what the sound might mean and how they feel as the ground begins to shake.'

The children now begin to work in role as river people, doing their daily tasks. You freeze the action every so often to hear their thoughts as they realise that the village is threatened by the volcano.

KS2

The teacher narrates:

'The Islanders have seen the strange large boat, floating off shore. At night, they gather round the fire and speak bravely of what it might be.' You then freeze the drama to create a class Still Picture (see above). Then, add a further piece of narration which asks the children to think more critically: 'That's what they're saying, but what are they thinking?

'Each of you take a moment to go over your secret thoughts about the strange floating shape a little way out at sea.

'If I touch you on the shoulder, be ready to speak your thoughts out loud if you want to.'

Teaching points

The 'if you want to' is very important. Try to work against the idea of this being a performance or a 'right or wrong' situation. It is simply a way of deepening the drama, of adding an extra layer. Let the class become accustomed to the idea that any child can 'pass' by remaining silent.

Use the strategy to go beyond the superficial. The formality of the way it is organised helps to focus minds, with less opportunity for showing off than in, for example, 'Small Group Playmaking' (see below).

You can also use Speaking Thoughts as a way of gauging the group's involvement and commitment to a piece of work. After the fun of making some Still Pictures, you could use this strategy to give an indication of the class's depth of thought about the situation.

Touching individuals on the shoulder is one way of eliciting thoughts. You can also sit down together and ask for thoughts or let individuals speak out loud in their own time. Many children find it surprisingly easy to create long sequences of talk when asked to do it in monologue style.

Development

Get yourself and your group used to the idea that you can use this strategy at any time within a drama session. It can be used from within almost any other strategy:

— when watching the results of Small Group Playmaking, stop the action with a 'FREEZE' at a particular point of interest, and then ask each person in turn to speak their thoughts from within the drama.

— let the children question you about your role's thoughts as you work using Teacher-in-role (see above).

— use the strategy within movement work, '...and as you're about to break through the tunnel to freedom, freeze absolutely still. What are you thinking......'

and so on.

Use the strategy retrospectively:

'Now think back to what's just happened. What were you thinking about as you....'

Let other class members speak the thoughts of an individual, 'What is Sara thinking as she waits for her brother. Can anyone speak her thoughts for us?'

A version of this which involves the whole class is known as 'Conscience Alley'.

The class forms two lines facing each other. A role or roles from the drama walk between the lines, and as they pass, each child in the lines offers advice on what the role(s) should do, in effect acting as the conscience of the role(s).

This works best when there is a clear dilemma.

- Should Michelle and Sean attempt to buy fireworks?
- Should Julie tell the teacher about the playground fight?
- Should Icarus make his first attempt at flight?

This can be fine-tuned so that those in one line offer advice about why the role *should* take a certain course, while those opposite say why they should not.

Encourage the children to give reasons for their advice, perhaps even to speak as a 'nagging conscience':

'...go on, no-one will know...'

'...it'll all be over in a second...'

'...it won't hurt them not to know the truth...'

'...you know you should tell, or James will get into trouble...'

'...just be honest, you know it's the best thing...'

'...you want to do it, you're ready for it now...'

As they emerge from walking through the lines, let the role(s) say what they have decided.

You can re-run this several times with discussion in between to deepen the arguments.

Small Group Playmaking

This is a form of prepared improvisation with the emphasis on presenting a situation to, and sharing ideas with, the rest of the class.

Examples

KS1

In work on 'Other lands', focus on a travel agency and let small groups create a scene where they ask about departure times, the weather at the destination, languages, money and so on. Have they thought of everything?

KS2

In your drama about the colonisation of a new planet, groups have to report on how they spent their first night on the planet. Using Small Group Playmaking, set each group the task of showing one incident from the first night by enacting it for the rest of the class to see. You might stress the need to choose an incident that can easily be presented in this form so that a tense harvesting and listing of strange fruits would be more impressive than a complicated tale involving invisible aliens!

Teaching points

The freedom that this strategy offers can lead to a lack of structure and organisation, so it is important to have the task and its parameters clearly defined. Do this by laying down clear guidelines before the groups start to work. In the example above, note that the groups are asked for one incident only and that suggestions are given as to the most appropriate scenario.

Suggest that each group discusses and agrees what their starting point will be and which roles they will adopt before enacting the drama.

Decide to what extent you want this to be purely experiential as opposed to performance based. If the latter, your motive would be the sharing of ideas in a dramatic form, so you might need to suggest that the groups choose the best moments from their improvisation and prepare these ready for sharing.

Don't compel groups to share their pieces, but if you find that some children are always reluctant, you could encourage them by asking them to explain what happened in their scene and to show one incident in the form of a Still Picture (see above).

Development

Stop the scenes at appropriate points to deepen the class's understanding by using Speaking Thoughts or class discussion.

Use the scenes as the starting point for further work. Ask the class to pitch in with suggestions for what would happen if:

- they did decide to go to the Head Teacher;

- they do offer to help the enemy;

- the giant does agree to let them in.

In other words, try out different versions of the same scene, following a variety of options. Let the same 'actors' enact the modified scene or swap over to let other class members try out their ideas (see Forum Theatre below).

It is sometimes useful to 'spotlight' random groups when using this form - perhaps by standing near to a group for a short time, then moving to another and so on. When you stand next to a group, they bring their scene to life, until you move on. This adds a useful tension to the showing of work and prevents restlessness amongst those who are waiting.

Sound Pictures

This is a method of evoking a place or situation by recreating its sounds or creating a collage of sounds which reflect different aspects of that place or situation.

Examples

KS1

'What sounds might you hear in the forest at night?'

Following a discussion, you can ask the class to create a whole-class sound picture.

'What sounds do we hear at a birthday party?'

'What sounds do we hear at the carnival?'

KS2

In the drama, the evacuees are leaving the city and heading out to the country for the first time. First, you discuss the different sounds they would hear, then you ask the class to vocalise the sounds of each place.

Teaching points

This can be a surprisingly effective way of setting the scene, and helping children to focus on the drama.

There are clear links with music here - why not create the forest scene above using percussion as well as vocal sounds?

It can help the children to recall what they know of certain eras or events, for example a sound collage of a wagon train in America.

Development

Create contrasting sound pictures by dividing the class into two groups (for example - one group takes City Sounds - the other Country Sounds). You conduct the groups, bringing them in at different times, thus forming a sound collage.

Make use of the School Radio drama programmes which often have rich sound backgrounds that can form a starting point or give support (see Appendix F).

Movement

This is any situation which requires 'as if' movement, where the participants imagine themselves to be in a given setting and move accordingly. Movement can be over used, because it seems safe, often requiring no interaction between class members. Used sparingly, however, it can deepen involvement in the drama and lead to more realistic and purposeful interaction, particularly in difficult scenes which involve confrontation or disaster, that can be dealt with using slow motion.

Examples

KS1+2

Working in pairs, children have been asked to find their way out of the Labyrinth, but they can only communicate by gesture, being as silent as possible. One leads, the other follows.

KS2

Groups create a movement sequence to a piece of music, showing how they travelled back in time.

Teaching points

Most movement work requires a sense of tension for its effectiveness. The Labyrinth example above, with its emphasis on stealthy, careful movement, will lead to a greater sense of involvement, particularly if followed by Speaking Thoughts or a whispered conversation on the first sighting of the Minotaur.

Although movement can be used for performance, it is also a powerful way of creating the shared world of the drama. For example:

◆   a group of elders is showing the newcomers around the village;

- we practise walking in our space suits before landing on the planet;

- together we walk through the undergrowth, ever watchful for those who might be tracking us!

Development

Movement need not be silent; talk in role often becomes most natural when focused on a movement task.

- 'as you work in the mine, talk quietly together about your plans for escape'.

Forum Theatre

Forum Theatre brings together many elements of Small Group Playmaking, Teacher-in-role, Speaking Thoughts and other strategies.

In this form of drama, certain members of the class take on roles and enact a situation whilst the rest watch. Those watching are active participants, however, and are able to stop the drama, make suggestions and even take over the roles, with a certain amount of guidance. They may ask what someone is thinking, suggest how they might react differently or ask to see the scene re-run from a particular point with a different emphasis. Actors can swap with watchers to try out different ideas with different people.

The most effective starting point for Forum Theatre is to begin with a dilemma or problem.

Examples

KS1

How can a small group welcome a new person into the class? Do they show her where everything is? Are they friendly and helpful? Stop the action and let other members of the class put in their own ideas, or take on roles as appropriate.

KS2

Can Mahinda persuade his parents to let him go on a school camp? With class members in role as parents, child and sister, the discussion begins. You let it run for a while, with an agreement that anyone with something to say about the progress of the discussion may raise their hands. When a few hands are in the air you halt the scene and hear comments. Take the various suggestions and change the development of the scene. If appropriate, let the watchers speak directly to the players:

'Rashinara, I don't think a mum would say that.'

But don't allow the watchers to make unsupported statements, they should justify their views. If you think it appropriate ask one of the watchers who has challenged something to swap places with one of the players. Alternatively, ask the players to swap roles within the enactment.

You have the full gamut of drama strategies available to help clarify and deepen the enactment. For example:

- *Speaking Thoughts:* 'Before we change what he says, let's hear what Dad was thinking at the point where we stopped the drama'.

- *Still Pictures:* 'Let's see a Still Picture showing each of them after the argument, what are they doing and what sort of mood are they in?'

- *Discussion:* 'Does it make any difference if it's Mahinda's sister who wants to go on the trip?'

Teaching points

The use of space is important here. Sitting in a circle with the enactment taking place in the middle can be very effective. What is vital, however you set up the space, is that everyone is close enough to the 'action' to feel involved.

This is a very powerful strategy, but it does require some experience of using drama to ensure that the whole class feels able to participate in some way. Otherwise it can become a forum for those who like acting in front of others. Fortunately, as a strategy it builds on all other forms of drama, so that children will gradually become equipped to use Forum Theatre as they work together using drama.

Development

Use Forum Theatre as a way of introducing a topic or theme. Talk through the situation, engaging the children's interest and giving opportunities for them to feed in their ideas, then move into Forum Theatre as a way of opening up the theme in drama. For example, during work on volcanoes, talk about people living in the shadow of a volcano which looks as if it might erupt. Then begin your Forum Theatre with a family deciding whether to leave the area - their home - or take the chance of staying. As the work develops you and the class can feed in extra factors to consider:

- it is harvest time, if you go now you'll lose the crops;

- the children have always wanted to move to the city anyway;

- some of the family are disabled, any journey would be hard for them.

Then move on to using other drama strategies to develop the situation. A village meeting with everyone in role would be a good way to develop this, or perhaps a ritualistic telling of the story of a time long ago when the volcano first erupted.

Dramatic Playing

This is often a first step, particularly for very young children, in exploring a new situation and establishing a dramatic context but it is also of value across the whole primary age range. It involves enacting an imaginary situation, usually without a specific task or dilemma. The teacher sets up the context and then may join in by adopting a supportive role, but not intervening or structuring at this stage. The main purpose of the activity is to allow children time to settle into their new imagined context giving them the freedom to try out ways of speaking and moving, and to feel comfortable with the situation. Although there is no central dilemma or task, this need not mean that children will drift aimlessly about the space. Individual dilemmas will emerge, as will a variety of events and roles.

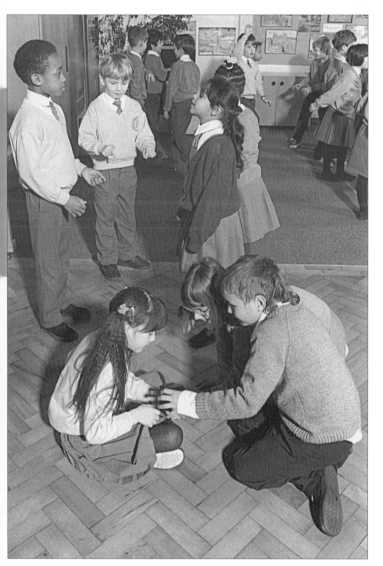

Examples

KS1

Children set up their market stalls and then begin trading. Some haggle over price, others try to keep neighbours quiet because their animals are disturbed. A refreshment stall becomes a focus for discussion about television, and so on.

KS2

Family groups are formed and roles shared out. Later the families in Allfolks St. will share a common dilemma, but for now, they are discovering one another's roles both within and between families. In one household an argument about bedtime erupts, in another they're celebrating a pools win, and so on.

Teaching points

Always give clear guidance as to the context of the Dramatic Play. In the Key Stage 1 example, children would probably need to talk first to establish a common view of what a market is and how it works. In the Key Stage 2 example, it might be important to give some indicators as to the nature of the context - no undercover police who will swoop on their neighbours and no households with occupants from another planet!

Be prepared to allow time for children to settle into the drama, to enjoy the play element, and to build up sufficient background for their role before moving on. It is often these Dramatic Play elements which engage and sustain a child's commitment to the unfolding drama.

Development

Having established the context through Dramatic Play, feed in a specific dilemma:

♦ one of the market traders is one hundred years old today, can we organise a secret party without him or her knowing? The teacher could adopt the role of the one-hundred-year-old, the preparations can only happen when she is not near your stall. This could develop as whole group drama (see below), and use a wide range of drama forms such as Still Pictures, Small Group Playmaking, Movement and so on.

♦ the residents of Allfolks St. receive a letter telling them that the street must be demolished for a new motorway. Call the residents together for a public meeting.

When children feel secure in their dramatic play, it might be appropriate to have a brief look at each group or area in turn while the rest of the class watches and listens. It is important here not to require each section to have a beginning and end, but rather to focus for a few moments on what is happening. This can aid the sense of 'Our Community, Our Group, Us', as individuals gain a wider picture of the dramatic context.

Whole Group Drama

This is any situation in which all the children in the class enter into the drama and act out a fictitious situation in order to explore some dilemma, or a clear, specific focus, usually established by the teacher.

In form, this is close to Dramatic Playing, but the addition of a shared tension or dilemma, the sense that 'we have to travel into unknown situations together' can mean that many teachers are nervous of this kind of drama, wondering whether their class can sustain it or whether one or two children will wreck things by seizing an opportunity for disruption.

In reality, this strategy should be used like any other, when it is appropriate, and for as long or short a time as is required.

It needn't get out of control because all the teacher's usual control factors are still available, and there is the option of stopping at any time to talk together, or to continue to explore the situation through other drama strategies - 'Let's stop there for a moment, David. What were you thinking when I told the village what had happened?'.

Examples

KS1

Half the class as the Forest Dwellers meet the other half, the River Bank People, for the first time. How will they show that they are friendly? The teacher is in role as the one who chairs the meeting.

KS2

The villagers meet to decide the fate of the family caught stealing. The teacher is in role as the villager who feels the level of poverty justifies the crime.

Teaching points

Whole Group Drama can take place with the whole group working together or splitting for a time into small groups, for example each village family decides on the thieves' fate before bringing their recommendations to the village meeting.

Always be clear whether you are expecting Whole Group Drama, or Small Group Playmaking (you do not, of course, have to use these terms). Do you want children to work in groups to produce something to share with the rest of the class - a television advert for example; or are you asking groups to continue to enact the situation as if it is happening now?

In the first case, the groups will need to plan, choose parts, practise and prepare a performance with an audience in mind. In the second case, they will move straight into the task, and will continue in role until you bring the task to an end.

Development

As your class gains experience, try starting work on a new theme in this way:

> Give an initial stimulus (a bundle of clothes or a half-finished letter).
>
> Give an initial role (villagers in a time before electricity in the days when people believed in magic).
>
> Give an initial sentence or two in role ('It's happened again! More of my sheep have gone, but this time, I found these old clothes stuck on my fence. Now how do you suppose they got there?')

Use this as the starting point for work on rumour and suspicion.

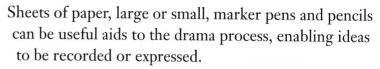

Drama on paper

Sheets of paper, large or small, marker pens and pencils can be useful aids to the drama process, enabling ideas to be recorded or expressed.

One of the most common uses is to take a large sheet of paper and have a child lie down on it while a couple of others draw around her outline. This shape can then become the role on which the group focuses.

Examples

KS1

'Satnam is going to be our zoo keeper. What does a zoo keeper have to do? Can you think of any jobs she might do in a day?'

As the children offer suggestions, the teacher writes them down around the outline.

Alternatively, talk about all the ideas, then ask the children to draw them and stick their drawings around the figure.

KS2

'What do we know about Guy Fawkes - any words or phrases that spring to mind when we think of him?'

The 'role' (picture on the paper) is then gradually surrounded by the children's suggestions - Fireworks, Gunpowder, November, Treason and so on.

As a focus on role

As things emerge about a role, so they are jotted down and kept for reference. Information and ideas can be kept on the wall and made available for all to see and refer to.

Examples

KS1

'What's the giant's favourite food? Let's have a look at the list on the picture we made.'

KS2

'Would Tom the Rat Catcher be brave enough to do that? Let's look at what we know he's done so far. Is there anything written down about him that suggests how he might behave now?'

As an aid to planning

To help build a shared picture of the drama, children can draw maps, plans, posters and other material which will be used within the drama.

Examples

KS1

'We want to make the airport as welcoming as possible, can you write or draw signs that will tell people where everything is, and make the place look as bright and cheery as possible?'

KS2

In work on travelling fairs, you have reached a point where local residents are complaining of too much noise. A small group could draw a plan showing where all the various rides are situated in the fairground. Another group could plan the local area showing the proximity of the fair to houses, shops, etc. A third group could create posters and banners protesting about the noise.

All of the above could be used as 'evidence' in the drama meeting which is to follow.

Teaching points

Don't be afraid to integrate work of this type into drama. Use writing or drawing if it is the best way to address a set of questions, or to add structure to the work. Some children will prefer to explore an area solely through active drama, but using writing and drawing helps to identify drama as part of the curriculum, to be valued and worked at.

Drama will often be the stimulus for a whole range of work that happens outside your drama sessions. For example, as children work on history, perhaps reading, listening to teacher, or perhaps on a museum trip, ask them to keep a note of any ideas, stories or people that might be useful in future drama work.

Narration

Narration can be used in a variety of ways and the term includes the breadth of spoken story-telling and scene-setting activities.

The key strengths of Narration are:

In setting up an initial context

KS1

'Everyone in Grimetown is asleep, but soon, when the people hear the whistle, they will have to drag themselves out of bed and go to work.'

KS2

'Can you imagine a town where the people who live on one side of the canal don't speak to those on the other side?'

As a bridge to move the drama on

KS1

'The factory owner decides that she can do without people altogether, she'll run her factory with her puppets.'

KS2

'In just one week the wall is built. It is so high that no one can see over it.'

As a way of dealing with potentially chaotic or even dangerous parts of a drama

KS1

'So the puppets went wild. They kicked at the machines and they jerked about on their strings but they just couldn't break free.'

'The two gangs met in no-one's land. At first they stood and looked at each other. Then, one of the Canal Street boys picked up a rock and threw it. In no time at all the air was full of flying stones, rocks and bottles.'

As a co-operative story-telling activity

'What do you think happened next? Who can tell us the next part of the story?'

'In your groups sit in a circle and take it in turns to describe the scene after the fight. You might add just one word or a sentence or two'.

Narration can be the prelude to a drama activity, it can accompany the activity (particularly when used to support movement), or it can be the activity as described in the story telling example above.

As a way of helping the class to reflect on the drama

'Lia knew that what the villagers had decided was wrong, but she kept her thought to herself and slowly walked away from the burning pile of waste.'

'She left the family wagon to search for food, knowing that she might not be able to find her way back in the dark. But the family's needs were great.'

Teaching points

Narration can simply be your usual way of explaining something, or it can be more formal, delivered with greater projection. It can be useful to have both styles available, adopting the second for work in the hall or when the children are spread out. The advantage of the 'formal voice' is that it gives a clear indication of the mode in which you are working, implying that 'this is part of the drama'.

Children can develop their own narration skills and may be encouraged to employ narration when they work on Small Group Playmaking.

Practical material
Pre-school

Bruin the Bear

Learning focus

To give the children a unique opportunity to have control of a social situation in which they give advice and suggestions. The focus of the drama is to explore the concept of uncertainty.

Curriculum links

- Story-building

- Problem-solving

- Language development

- Follow-up work in painting, drawing and name-writing.

Context

This is a drama session where the children do not need to go into role, but can remain as themselves, in giving advice to a toy bear who does not understand why he has been sold as a birthday or Christmas present.

It has been planned for use by a teacher working in tandem with a nursery nurse, parent or friend. For the sake of clarity, we have assumed that the teacher is facilitating and leading the lesson and the other adult is in role as Bruin.

We would not suggest any elaborate costume or 'larger than life' acting skills as this could prove threatening for the children and lead to them adopting a passive audience role.

Preparing the role

The teacher gathers the children in a quiet corner of the nursery and explains that together they are going to make a special story. It is explained that the nursery nurse is going to have a very important role in the story, by pretending to be a toy bear called Bruin. The nursery nurse can then put on a simple costume in front of the children (it needs to be simple: perhaps a bow-tie or a waistcoat). The children will need to see his face in order to be able to judge how Bruin is feeling.

The nursery nurse then sits down, looking very fed up, with a specially-made 'SOLD' sign round his neck.

Facilitating the questions

Individual teachers will know how best to get their children to talk, but an effective strategy is to bring the bear to life or freeze him with a click of the fingers. In this way, the teacher remains in control of the focus and can guide the children's questions. For example:

> **Teacher:** What do you think is wrong with Bruin?

> **Teacher:** When I click my fingers we can see Bruin waiting in the toy-shop. How do we think he is feeling?

> **Teacher:** Let's ask Bruin some questions and see if we can help.

> **Teacher:** Let's hear what Bruin is thinking in our story.

The problem

The nursery nurse and teacher will have to decide how much time they want to spend with the children speculating, before giving the children the precise reason for Bruin's sadness, which is:

> **Nursery nurse (*as Bruin*):** I've been sold as a present and I don't know what it means!

> I overheard the toy-shop manager telling someone on the telephone!

The problem now is with the children: teachers can decide if they want Bruin to be a Christmas or a birthday present.

Teacher: Will you help?

How?

Who can explain to Bruin what happens when a toy is sold?

Who can explain what might happen at the birthday party?

Helping Bruin

A pretend birthday party can now take place to show Bruin what kinds of things might happen:

i) delivering Bruin to the house by van or post;

ii) unwrapping Bruin;

iii) singing 'Happy Birthday', blowing candles out and making a wish;

iv) games like 'dead lions', 'pass the parcel', and 'ring-a-ring-a-roses';

v) asking a child to pretend to be the one whose party it is (ask if it is really someone's birthday in the class).

Conclusion

The end of the session will need to be judged carefully by the teacher. We recommend that the children succeed in making Bruin happy and that the drama draws to an end with Bruin waiting contentedly in the toy shop window and looking forward to being collected. The real learning will have taken place in exploring Bruin's uncertainty through concepts like 'sold', 'birthday' and 'surprise', and it is important that children at this age have satisfactory and happy resolutions.

A final song could bring the session to a close: perhaps 'If you're happy and you know it'. It is very important that the adult in role as Bruin takes off the items of costume and indicates to the children that the story has come to an end and he is now out of role.

Send for the doctor

Learning Focus

To create opportunities for the children to advise and observe the consequences of that advice.

Curriculum links

◆ Language use

◆ Social skills in working together, using the telephone, and dealing with problems in the immediacy of the drama.

Context

This is a drama session based within the context of ill-health, which children of this age understand. It is planned for the teacher to be involved in the drama, with one or two dolls in role as babies!

The context is designed to encourage the children to use their knowledge about baby-care, and to spur them to suggest ways of dealing with unexpected events. The lesson is written with the general acknowledgement that this is likely to be the children's first group drama experience.

Preparation

Some time will need to be given to preparation, particularly the way the space is prepared. Nursery children do not always find it easy to be part of a large group and it might be wise to restrict this drama to between eight and ten children.

In a quiet area of the nursery put one or two dolls to bed, making sure that the children who are going to participate have a good position from which to see the dolls and to take part easily, if they so wish.

Contract making

Gather the children together and explain: 'Today, we are going to make a special story together! In the story, I am going to play at being a mum with two children. All you need to do at first is to watch. We will pretend that the two dolls here are my two children.'

Enactment by teacher-in-role.

Once the children are clear that all they need to do is to watch, you will need to put on a piece of clothing to show that you are going into role as Mum: perhaps a coat, scarf or hat.

As Mum, your face shows how anxious you are at this opening point in the story, and you talk aloud to yourself so that the children can begin to get a sense of what is happening. The children watch and read the situation. You could say something like this:

'Oh! dear, Oh! dear, I'm sure I don't know what to do! Both of them in bed and not making a sound. I wonder if they're asleep?'

As Mum, you now creep into the bedroom of the two children, take a peep at them, confirming that they are still asleep and tip-toe out again, with a big sigh.

Discussion

As soon as you're out of the room, take off the clothing and ask the children what kind of things they saw or noticed about the story.

It is very important that, in your discussion, you always refer to 'The mum in the story' or 'The children in the story', in order that the class are aware of the definition of fiction and reality.

Suggested leading questions:

'How was the Mum in the story feeling, do you think?'

'Is it unusual for children to sleep as soundly as the children in the story? Do you?'

'What do you think the Mum in the story should do?'

Finally...

'I'll give you the chance to talk to her'.

Hot-seating

Explain to the children that you are going to become Mum again, by putting the clothing back on. Sit on a special stool or chair, which 'marks' you as different to the children, and encourage them to ask you questions.

You can make this as easy, or as hard, as you wish. Some examples:

Class: What's wrong with them?

    Mum: I don't know.

Class: What are their names?

    Mum: Lee and Karen.

Class: Do they go to school?

    Mum: Well, the Nursery.

Class: Are they ill?

    Mum: I don't know.

Class: Wake them up!

    Mum: I don't think I should – they stayed up very late last night.

Class: Did they watch telly last night?

    Mum: Yes.

Class: Why? Etc.

Discussion

Take off the clothing again, leave the stool, and facilitate further discussion, the key question being:

'What should this Mum do?'

It is now up to you as teacher to decide whether to explain that the children in the story are unwell - although we suspect that many classes will already have suggested this. However, it can be frustrating to allow a guessing game to develop and if you have pre-planned what you want to focus on, then it is only fair to let the children know.

Teacher-in-role

You can now go back into role and, after listening to the advice of the class, put their ideas into action. You can decide if you want these ideas, suggestions and advice to work.

Some possible courses of action:

a) **Class:** Why don't you phone the Doctor?

    Mum: All right, but will you help me?

(Class can make the call for Mum, on an imaginary or play phone, whilst Mum cares for her two children in bed.)

b) **Class:** Wake them up and ask them what is wrong.

   Mum: All right - will you come with me and help?

(Two of the class volunteer to be the 'voices' of the two sick children, standing behind the dolls and speaking the dialogue for them. A conversation can then take place between Mum and her children.)

c) **Class:** They are very ill.

   Mum: Oh, dear me! I'm ever so worried!

(Teacher now explains that she is going to freeze as the Mum in the story and the class have to say what's going on in her head at this serious moment.)

d) **Class:** Give them a cuddle!

   Mum: But there are two of them. Will you help?

(The class, or representatives from the class, demonstrate how to wake the children up, take them out of bed and give them a cuddle.)

There are many other possibilities for how this might develop. You can make suggestions yourself, or simply wait for the children to come up with ideas, which might involve:

— giving the 'children' breakfast;

— medicine;

— doctor comes;

— a hospital visit;

— telling the family about the illness;

— making them better and playing games with them;

— taking them to Nursery and having a drink of orange with them.

Conclusion

We do recommend that, no matter which of the areas becomes the focus, you should structure for a happy ending, since this is likely to be the children's first drama experience.

It would seem a good idea to use songs or games with which the class is familiar to sing with the dolls in a whole group context.

Key Stage 1

Five- to six-year-olds

A quilt of feelings

Learning focus

To develop the children's grasp of old age, highlighting its celebratory qualities, particularly within the family context.

Curriculum links

- Art and design
- Personal and social education
- Writing

Context

This drama has been adapted from a sequence of lessons, which began when a child brought her pattern-making to school to show her teacher at 'sharing time'. The pattern,

created on a small piece of paper in felt-tip, was discussed by the whole class, who said it reminded them of a patchwork quilt. The class teacher then developed the children's ideas into a drama upon which the following is based. It could be exciting for the children to find a way of constructing a quilt, to which they keep adding as each drama is experienced. This could be a feature in the classroom and help to sustain interest.

We strongly recommend the book *The Patchwork Quilt* by Valerie Flournoy (Puffin Books).

Drama forms

Teacher-in-role

Aim: to introduce the drama procedures to the children, and to stimulate their interest in an older person. Gather the children together in a quiet area, at a time when you feel confident that you will have at least thirty minutes of undisturbed time!

Explain to the children that you are going to pretend to be a woman called Edna for a short time and that their task will be to find out as much as they possibly can about Edna.

Remember: Edna can be re-introduced at any time, sometimes with money as a focus, or homes, or memories, or people who help us. Edna is a living teaching resource for all curriculum areas, once effectively established.

There are two simple rules:

i) When you put on the shawl, you will speak only as Edna; after you take it off, you will be yourself again.

ii) None of the class need act, but simply ask questions of Edna, as themselves, and therefore the usual system of 'hands up' can still apply.

Before putting on the shawl, it would be best to talk about Edna, explaining that she is elderly and that the children will need to be gentle with her. This avoids the children getting into a pointless guessing game. They will be aware of the kind of person they are going to meet and will begin to anticipate and prepare some potential questions.

Once the shawl is on and Edna is seated, she explains that she is making a patchwork quilt showing different events from her life, making each piece of the quilt reflect particular feelings. The children should soon get into the task and be quickly asking questions that interest them:

For example:

How old are you?
Where do you live?
Do you have any children?
What is a quilt?
Are you feeling sad now?
Are you lonely?

At any point that the questions become difficult to answer, don't hesitate to stop, take off the shawl and discuss the particular difficulty with the children. Don't prolong the role-play simply for the sake of it.

As Edna, you can build into the drama any events or information which you feel your class would be interested in or which would link to other topics. You can introduce aspects of Edna's life-style which best suit your teaching purpose.

For example:

- Edna can have a lot of relatives, or a few.

- Edna can have any income level you choose.

- She can live anywhere in the country, in any style of house. She can follow any kind of lifestyle.

It is also important to create a sense of Edna's childhood home, and for the teacher in role to describe incidents which happened there.

When you think there is little more to be developed, then bring the questioning to a close and take off the shawl. Perhaps it would be best to write down some of the information about Edna (see 'Drama on Paper', page 68, for ways of doing this).

Circle time

Aim: to develop individual self-esteem by acknowledging the qualities of each child in the class.

This strategy may appear to be diverting the focus away from Edna, initially.

The children are seated in a formal circle and you have prepared a small piece of card, which has a rectangle cut out of the middle, making a frame. This piece of card is passed around the circle and each child holds it in front of their face. The rest of the class say the kinds of qualities this person has and which of these qualities would be present if the class were to make their own patchwork quilt.

For instance, the children might say:

'Gareth's hair is really nice'

'Tom is always smiling'

'Helen's a good drawer'.

You record all the comments in readiness for the quilt that will be made later.

Connections between the kind of qualities being identified amongst the children and the feelings which developed from questioning Edna are best made by teachers in their own way, but some possible ideas are:

— make two lists on large paper, written by the teacher, with the headings:

Edna's feelings   Feelings within our class

Collective drawing

On one large roll of paper, ask the children to draw images or put words which depict Edna's feelings, on another, show the feelings which were evident in the circle time.

Whole-group drama

Aim: to highlight the importance of the past and to compare youth with older age.

In this strategy, the children are asked to go back in time with Edna, as she explains some of her strong childhood memories. In reality, the children can make almost all of the decisions, with the teacher in role as Edna supporting their ideas.

A) Setting up the drama

i) Define the space which will represent Edna's childhood bedroom, perhaps by chairs or chalk.

ii) Explain that when the drama goes back in time you will place Edna's shawl around your waist to represent a skirt.

iii) Explain that each child, or groups of children, can now describe one thing which they think is in Edna's home. The way in which they do it is to step into the defined space, speaking aloud what they can see in their 'mind's eye'.

In this way, the children are using the information they have gleaned from Edna and are also making their imagined images more fixed and believable.

B) Doing the drama

The next stage is the crucial one, as far as whole-group drama is concerned.

Teacher: I would now like all of you to become Edna's friends when she was a little girl. They used to play different kinds of games, sometimes in the street, sometimes in the house. Some games you already know.

I'm putting the shawl around my waist to show you that I'm now the same age as you.

(Re-arrange the shawl and step into the space)

Hello everyone! I'm really pleased you're all here. Let's play 'Oranges and Lemons!'

This is a sequence for focusing on childhood games, but you might want to develop it in another way that you feel is best for your class. You may want to focus on:

- street-games
- Christmas
- birthdays
- falling-out with special friends
- getting into trouble with Mum or Dad
- jobs around the home.

Any of these can be introduced in one of the following ways:

— by the teacher, as young Edna, introducing it in the drama context;

— by the teacher stopping the drama, explaining some of the things children did at that time;

— by the teacher returning to old Edna and describing her childhood in more detail.

C) Reflecting on the drama

When you feel that you have worked long enough in this whole-group drama, it is now important to reflect with the children. Ask them to return to the quiet area where they will meet old Edna again. She asks the children how they think she should show the episodes from her youth, in the quilt. She leads a discussion about the differences in the lifestyle then and now.

Making the Quilts

Teachers will know how best to make the quilts which can become features of the classroom displays, but some simple ideas are:

i) make a large rectangle on one wall, and each time an episode takes place with Edna, a group of children make a further piece of the quilt to be added to the whole.

ii) use felt material which can have pictures chalked on it.

iii) make a quilt of pictures and a quilt of writing.

Playgrounds

Learning focus

Working together

Collective decision-making

Curriculum links

- P.E.

- Personal, social and health education.

- There are also possible links with art, technology, maths and writing. See 'How to use the material', below.

Context

The children are faced with making decisions about a new playground for their area, a subject in which they are the acknowledged experts. The strength of exploring this through drama is that they have to agree together and work pragmatically in order to see an end result.

How to use the material

The material could be used in one forty-minute session or split up over a number of shorter working periods. It lends itself to integration into writing and artwork. Drawing a plan of the new playground is an obvious link, but you could also consider writing a list of items required. A model of the proposed playground would also give opportunities for work in design and technology.

Drama forms

Discussion

Aim: to begin to focus on the many uses of playgrounds.

As a class group, talk about playgrounds the children know and and how they are used. Record the results on a large piece of paper or a board.

Teaching points

Have we thought of every possible use for playgrounds?

- Playing on your own or with friends

- Playing sports

- Imaginary games

- Playing on the apparatus

- Having a picnic

- Using the playground as a meeting place

Draw this together by choosing one playground that most of the class knows. It would be good if this was one which really did have some room for improvement, rather than a new or very well equipped playground.

Alternatively, present the class with pictures you have drawn of an imaginary playground, or a simple ground plan.

Showing the playground in action

Aim: to use Still Pictures to enable groups to focus in detail on one of the playground's uses.

Agree together on what the playground is like, what equipment it has and so on. You could extend this into making plans of the playground as it is now.

Ask the children to work in groups. They are to choose one of the playground's uses and present it in a clear, exciting Still Picture. Allow just a few minutes for working these out and then share them in turn. Let other members of the class describe what is happening in each picture as they look at it.

Teaching points

Are there small details in the pictures that can be drawn out
and commented upon? These might be quite subtle elements
which add a sense of realism and life to the pictures - a child
crying, a mum hurrying her children - and so on.

Do any of the pictures tell a story?

Planning the new playground

Aim: to focus on how the playground could be improved.

Explain that you are going to pretend that a group called the
New Playground Organisation has asked if any children in the
area would like any changes to be made to nearby playgrounds.

In their groups, the children have to come up with a suggestion
for one improvement to the playground.

Development: this would be a good opportunity to introduce
artwork into the session, asking groups to produce an image of
their improvement to show to the rest of the class in the next
activity.

Teaching points

As you go from group to group, focus on any practical
problems associated with the improvements.

For example, is there room for the proposed climbing frame?
Would it be safe for all children? Are there any features that
would help children with disabilities?

Use this questioning to encourage the children to think
through their plans more deeply in preparation for the meeting
below.

Meeting

Aim: to use Teacher-in-role to facilitate reporting back on the
small-group work above. Using Teacher-in-role will give an
added tension to the reporting back - the ideas have to be well
expressed in order to impress someone from outside the
school. Using this strategy will lead to a greater involvement in
the issue.

Explain to the class that they are all going to come to a
meeting with somebody from the New Playground
Organisation, and that you are going to be the person from the

organisation. During the meeting, everyone can put forward their plans. The New Playground Organisation only has a small amount of money to spend on all the playgrounds in the country, so the children will have to try to convince you that their ideas really are needed.

It will help if you set up a space for the meeting. A small class could meet sitting around some tables which have been pushed together, or you might meet in your story area. Wherever the meeting takes place, give it a sense of occasion and a certain formality. Explain to the children that the meeting will start when you enter/sit.

Begin the meeting by formally introducing yourself and explaining its purpose. Then hear the plans, asking the children to be brief and clear. You can use your role to elicit more information and to get the children to argue their case more strongly. The role involves not knowing the area and so you can ask questions which the teacher would not need to:

> You mean there's a great river rushing through the playground, isn't that rather dangerous?

Child: We call it a river, but it's only small, about this wide.

Move through this fairly quickly and then thank the group, saying that you will send a letter shortly giving your decision.

Teaching points

Are any of the ideas similar enough to be merged?

Do the children want to change or adapt any of their ideas now that they have heard from everyone?

Don't be afraid to drop role for discussion.

Waiting to hear

Aim: to use Speaking Thoughts to explore the experience of waiting to hear some important news.

Explain that it is the morning that the letter from the New Playground Organisation is due to arrive. Ask the class to imagine that it is just before school starts. They are to take up an appropriate position - lining up, hanging up coats or whatever they are used to. Start this as a class Still Picture in order to give some shape and structure, then bring it to life to create a Living Picture. Use narration to take the children through the activity. An example is given below, but you should make the words your own, and fit them to your school situation.

As you stand in line, waiting to go in, perhaps you feel a bit cold. If you do, let that show in how you stand and in your movements.

Then you remember, today is a special day, the day when you hear if all your plans for the playground are to go ahead. What are you thinking and how do you feel?

Are you excited? Nervous? Happy? Worried?

Can you think of one word to describe how you are feeling and what you are thinking?

Then ask for hands up or touch people on the shoulder to hear their ideas (see page 54 for ways of using Speaking Thoughts).

Finally bring the narration and dramatic action to an end with the children coming into the classroom. At this point produce the letter (see below) and enter the drama yourself. Place the letter in a prominent position (perhaps on your desk), and ask the class to sit down as you have some important news.

The Letter

Aim: to foster negotiation, co-operation and group decision making.

Either photocopy the letter at the end of this section, or create your own version with details that are more specific to your class. Seal it in an official-looking envelope.

After establishing that you are in the drama with the children, ask a good reader to open the letter and read it to the class.

Re-read or explain anything which children find difficult to ensure that everyone understands the task which is that, as a class, they have to decide now on just one important project. It may be possible for other ideas to be done later, but for now, just one project must be chosen, and chosen today.

Now comes the difficult part as, in the discussion which follows, some children may not want to let go of their own ideas.

How will the class decide?

Will they talk through the most popular ideas until they reach a decision?

Will they use some other method of deciding such as a vote?

Are there any ideas which would benefit a greater number or be used more extensively? Should greater weight be given to these ideas?

The new playground

Aim: to represent the results of the decision-making through a Still Picture.

End the session by creating a class Still Picture showing the new playground, as agreed.

There are a number of ways of using this picture. You could ask children to speak thoughts or bring the picture to life for a few seconds before freezing again in a new position to represent the new playground in action.

You might adopt the role of a reporter from the local paper and interview the children about what they are doing and what they think of the new playground. If you took a small group at a time, they could show their part of the picture to the rest of the class who could then listen to the interview.

Children could think of headlines to accompany the pictures that appear in the local paper.

Teaching points

What makes the new playground so good?

Can anyone tell the story of how the new playground came about?

Was it hard to decide together?

The New Playground Organisation
23 Roundabout Villas
Slidetown
SW1 NGS

Dear Children,

Thank you very much for inviting me to your school the other day. I really enjoyed my visit and hearing all your ideas.

Many of your plans sounded exciting and I wish that we could help you to put all your ideas into action.

I am sorry to say that we have had such a large number of children wanting to improve their playgrounds, that we simply do not have enough money for everything. However, we have decided to give your playground one new thing.

We can only supply this if:
1. Everyone agrees on what the thing should be,
2. If you can let me know what you want straight away - today.
I hope that you can come up with a good idea - and soon.

Yours sincerely,

Ms. C. Saw.

1 Discussion

A class discussion on the the theme of Dragons. Seek to identify:

Stories in which Dragons appear,

Common ideas about dragons,

Differentiating between Dragons and Dinosaurs.

2 Still Pictures

In groups, make pictures of dragons, using the whole group together to be one dragon.

3 Living Pictures

Bring the pictures to life to show the dragon sleeping, feeding, angry, sad.

Snapshot Key Stage 1
Dragons

Learning focus

Are things always what they seem?

How do we form our ideas about what people will be like?

7 Enactment

Upon reaching the dragon, the class gently questions her. Let group members answer for the dragon or use teacher in role.

4 Sound Pictures

With the whole class, create Dragon Sounds to match the Living Pictures. Then use these for the rest of the class to vocalise as each group shows their pictures.

8 Still pictures 2

In groups:

i) What we thought the dragon would be like.

ii) What it is like.

6 Movement

Approaching the dragon.

Use music and/or narration from the teacher to create the atmosphere of approaching the sad dragon. Make the journey one which takes the children deep into the dragon's cave, with careful controlled movement. Freeze the action once or twice to hear spoken thoughts.

5 Speaking thoughts

Choose one of the Sad Dragon pictures. Ask the group that made it reform the picture while the rest of the class stand around it in a circle. Then let class members speak the thoughts of the dragon, thoughts which explain why the dragon is sad.

9 Discussion

How can we help the dragon? After discussion explore this through drawing, writing, Still or Living pictures, Teacher in role or Small Group Playmaking.

1 Stories

There are a wealth of stories which use children's fears and uncertainties as a starting point. Two lesser known examples are:

Who's afraid now? Rose Impey (BBC Longman) about a boy who is scared of bedtime in Granny's bedroom.

The train who was frightened of the dark Denis Bond (Hippo): a train learns to conquer fear of a tunnel.

There are also many fairy and traditional tales which touch on this theme, Little Red Riding Hood or hansel and Gretel for example.

Use stories as a way in to talking about dangerous places, encouraging children to offer any responses which relate to real or imaginary places. Where appropriate, try to draw out and identify the actual or perceived danger in each place.

2 Teacher-in-role

Explain that you, in role, are frightened of somewhere that you have to go to.

Before going into role, briefly discuss with the class how they would treat someone who is unhappy, nervous or frightened about something. Will they be able to help you to talk about your fears?

Now adopt your role: you are a child who is frightened of going to a new school, but you don't reveal this. Talk about the school in exaggerated terms - how it might appear to a fearful child's imagination. It is a big place. The people there are nasty to you. No one will be your friend. The people who run it don't tell you what to do and then tell you off because you don't know what to do... and so on.

Then come out of role and discuss with the children who you were and why you were frightened. Ask the question - Is school a dangerous place?

Snapshot Key Stage 1
Dangerous Places

Learning focus

Focusing on those places, both real and imaginary, which threaten or frighten children.

4 Enactment

Either you, or a class member, take on the role of the new child. The class has to welcome the child and make him or her feel at home in the classroom. Start with a class frozen picture as the new child stands by the door having just entered the class. Ask the whole class to suggest what the new child's thoughts might be at this moment.

Then bring the scene to life, stopping whenever a decision needs to be made - should we all crowd round like this? What would be the most helpful thing to do now? What things do we need to show Michelle to make her feel at home with us?

Don't be afraid to go back and try out different ideas.

Then let the new child tell the class her thoughts and feelings during her first day at your school.

3 Still Pictures

Having established that school wasn't as dangerous a place for the new child as she thought , go on to talk about real dangers at school.

Let the children share their responses freely, and then ask groups to create Still Pictures showing real dangers at school.

When you share the pictures, point out that most of these dangers can be dealt with if people are careful.

5 Posters

End with a discussion of really dangerous places that children should never visit alone.

Ask groups to design posters based on what you have talked about: a clear picture with, if appropriate, a clear slogan. These can either be done as drawings or as Still Pictures with headlines.

Key Stage 2

Seven- to nine-year-olds

Tricks and tricksters

Learning focus

Looking at and identifying 'trickster' characters from legends and literature.

Focusing on tricks that children play and asking the question: When does a trick become trouble?

Curriculum links

- English: reading, writing, speaking and listening.

- Personal, social and health education.

Context

By focusing on crafty characters that the children will already know (or that they will meet as you read and talk together), this section opens up the whole question of tricks and fun which might become annoyance and then trouble.

How to use the material

Use the ideas in this section to integrate drama into a book week or other work focusing on trickster characters such as Anansi, Brer Rabbit, Robin Hood, Finn and Oona, Gremlins.

At the end of this section we offer suggestions for how work growing out of this material can be used as a time of sharing or performance, perhaps for a school assembly or at a special event for parents.

Drama forms

Discussion

Aim: To encourage an interest in books and stories about tricksters.

Read or tell a trickster tale, perhaps an Anansi story, a Brer Rabbit story, a Beatrix Potter tale or part of the Robin Hood legend. It could be one of the Irish tales of the giant Finn and his clever wife Oona, or any of a multitude of traditional or modern stories.

Get the children to talk about the story in the usual way, then broaden the discussion to take in any trickster type tales that the children know. They may well include cartoons or comic book characters at this stage.

Story-telling and Still Pictures

Aim: to encourage the children to tell trickster tales, and to understand them by focusing on key moments. In groups, ask the children to choose a favourite trickster tale (or the one you have just told), to sit in a circle and tell the story with each child passing on to the next after a couple of sentences.

Then ask them, in their groups, to choose two special moments from the story, and to represent these moments in Still Pictures.

Share each group's pictures with the class and encourage discussion on why these particular pictures were chosen.

Teaching points

What is happening in each picture?

What other tricks is this character known for?

How does the person being tricked feel?

Why is Anansi/Oona/The Fox playing a trick on this person/animal? Have they done something to deserve it?

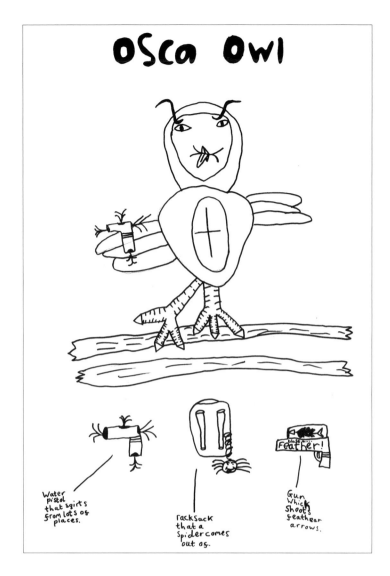

Drawing

Aim: to encourage children to develop characters of their own.

In groups, pairs or individually (whichever is best for your group at the time of working). Children draw their own made up trickster character on a large sheet of paper and juxtapose it with the trickster's characteristics.

Hot Seating

Aim: to share the ideas generated in the above exercise, and to add depth to the children's creations.

As a way of sharing ideas, let groups or individuals (as above), sit in the hot seat(s) and answer questions about their creation, as if they are the trickster character. They can have their drawings with them and can refer to them as appropriate.

Teaching points

Encourage questions which focus on the character's trickster nature.

What's your favourite kind of trick?

Do you have any special powers?

Do you trick anyone or just people you think deserve it?

Small Group Playmaking

An option here is to ask groups to enact a story showing their trickster in action.

Teaching points

Before you begin to work on your story, think about:

How will you show the "trick"? If it involves magic or special powers, do you have a way of letting us know what has happened?

Can you make your story short and clear, so that we know exactly what is going on and who everyone is?

What types of drama will you use in your story - Still Pictures, Speaking Thoughts, Storytelling, as well as acting it out?

Discussion and Small Group Playmaking/Speaking Thoughts.

Aim: to begin to think about tricks and tricksters from the children's own experience.

Now encourage the class to focus on tricks from their own experience, perhaps starting with Halloween or April Fools. Have they ever been tricked, or tricked someone else?

Move on to group work, where small groups enact a trick, showing what happens, who is tricked, how and why.

Give similar constraints and encouragements to those in the previous section and stress the careful action involved in setting up the trick, which will create dramatic tension.

Share each group's drama twice. The second time, freeze the action at significant moments to allow the roles to speak their thoughts.

Teaching points

How does the person being tricked feel?

Why are they the victim of this trick, do they deserve to be?

Is this trick just good fun, or is it turning into trouble?

Still Pictures

Aim: to draw out two aspects of tricks - fun and trouble. Working in the same groups, ask for two Still Pictures. Each picture has a title. Picture One is TRICKS CAN BE FUN.

Picture Two is TRICKS CAN BE TROUBLE.

Share the pictures and talk about them as a class.

Teaching points

Is the 'fun' picture fun for everyone involved?

Who is in trouble in the 'trouble' picture? Is anyone hurt, sad or upset?

What makes a trick good, what makes it fun?

How can you decide if a trick is going wrong?

Posters

As an optional development of the Still Pictures, working in groups or individually, ask the children to take a trickster character to use in a poster which sums up your work on tricks and tricksters. For example:

ANANSI SAYS: 'TRICKS CAN BE FUN, AND TRICKS CAN BE TROUBLE'.

Performance

In order to share this work with an audience, you could create a short performance based on the drama work that the class has undertaken. This could take many forms and would evolve alongside the classroom work. A suggested structure for the finished performance is given below.

1   Introduction from teacher. A brief outline of the class' work, the stories they read and how they began to think about Tricks and Tricksters. You should also be prepared to link the various sections with a brief word of explanation.

2   Extract from one of the trickster tales that the children have enjoyed. To emphasise the value placed on literature, read or have children read if appropriate, an extract or an abbreviated story, while different groups of children form Still Pictures which illustrate and comment upon it.

> **NOTE:**
> This will need careful rehearsal so that the children are able to move smoothly from picture to picture. Give a clear verbal signal for each group to move to, and rehearse enough for the children to feel confident without becoming over familiar or bored with the material. The linking of the pictures might be enhanced by percussion or a short recorded theme.

3   Show drawings of the children's own made-up tricksters. Choose one or two groups/individuals and interview them about their creations.

4   Enact a scene from one group's Small Group Playmaking which shows a trick from the children's own experience. The group which shows this will need a fair degree of rehearsal and support. If you feel uncertain about this activity, you could narrate while children show Still Pictures taken from their drama.

5   Freeze the action at a suitable point and let the characters in turn speak their thoughts, illustrating that how much you enjoy a trick depends on where you are in the trick!

6   End with the whole class repeating the slogan: TRICKS CAN BE FUN - accompanied by a whole class Still Picture illustrating this, and TRICKS CAN BE TROUBLE - again illustrated with a whole class Still Picture.

The story of Minik Peary Wallace

Learning focus

To examine some of the myths and misunderstandings about the lifestyle and identity of the Inuit people.

Curriculum links

- Human geography
- Lifestyles of other societies, past and present
- How myths are created
- How cultures impact on other cultures
- Drama structures

It is important that the children are free to express their initial thoughts at the beginning of the first session, in order that they can then reflect and evaluate the extent to which they have changed their views and understanding about Inuit culture.

Context

The Inuit culture of Greenland has suffered from the influences of Western civilisation, and this project is intended to give children a more realistic grasp of human geography by focusing on the life of one man.

The story of Minik is included here as it is essential that the children understand the events and dates at a relevant point in the project.

Drama forms

Word association game

The class is asked to work in groups of four or five to play a short word game. Starting from the word 'Eskimo' they say as many words as they can. This will only last a few minutes and is a way of sharing whatever information they already know. If the children cannot come up with anything at all, then use the photograph as a more concrete starting point.

Group mime

The same groups are now asked to create a 'film sequence' without dialogue called 'The Life of the Eskimo'.

As each of the groups present their work, the teacher asks the rest of the class to comment on such issues as occupations, activities or family life, which are being presented in the mime. The teacher writes them all down for subsequent analysis.

This simple drama structure will quickly inform the teacher about the children's attitudes and views towards Inuits.

Still images

The teacher now introduces a piece of factual information either verbally or in written form giving the children the definitions of two key words - Eskimo and Inuit. The teacher also explains that Inuit is the term by which a people of Greenland wants to be known.

Eskimo - eater of raw flesh

Inuit - the People

Following a brief discussion about the words and how they make the children feel, ask the groups to create Still Pictures which include their own interpretations of the two words, and their responses to them. Thus, Inuit and Eskimo are both presented in each group image.

The Still Images should provide rich material for a whole-group discussion about culture, about how names are arrived at, who gives or has given groups of people names, and where children get information about people from other lands.

— How can we be certain that that information is always accurate and correct? (For example, are all Australians like those on *Neighbours?*)

— How do stereotypes develop?

> **NOTE:**
>
> It would be advisable to pause the drama at this point, in order to give the children time to research some further information about the Inuit lifestyle today and in the past.

Discussion

There is a stark contrast between the Inuits' economic use of resources and, for example, the large-scale fishing undertaken at the same time by developed countries. The Inuits would fish or hunt one animal at a time and thus preserve their food supplies for a lengthy period of time.

Which is the most sensible environmentally?

Are the Inuits really the primitive society?

How would the Inuits have responded to this large-scale fishing?

The story of Minik

The teacher will need to read the story of Minik's life, to prepare for the next sequence of drama work.

THE STORY OF MINIK PEARY WALLACE

Minik was born in 1889. He was a Polar Eskimo (Inuit) and his home was in Etah, a small village in north-west Greenland. The village had a population of less than 250 people. His father, Qisuk, was considered to be one of the best hunters in the village. His mother had died when he was young.

In 1897, Robert Peary, who was on his fourth expedition to Greenland, took Qisuk on as hunter and dog driver and then invited him to travel south with him, back to New York. Minik travelled to New York with his father and six other Inuits. Peary promised to have them back home within a year.

The S.S. Hope, their ship, arrived in New York at the end of September, 1897. On that day alone, twenty thousand people visited the Hope to see 'the Eskimos'. Peary had really brought the Inuits to America at the request of Dr. Franz Boas, assistant curator at the American Museum of Natural History.

The group of Inuits were housed in the basement of the museum. The heat of New York was oppressive to the Inuit and living in a basement, they soon caught colds which developed into pneumonia. By November all six of them were in Bellevue Hospital.

In February 1898, Minik's father, Qisuk, died, and the Museum authorities apparently gave him an Inuit burial ceremony. With the exception of one, Visaahassak, all the others soon followed. Visaahassak returned to Greenland with Peary.

Meanwhile, Minik was living with William Wallace, Superintendent of the Museum, in New York. He had recovered from pneumonia although he was a victim of recurring bouts of the illness for the rest of his life. Wallace and his wife Rhetta doted on Minik and they adopted him and sent him to school, where arithmetic and sports were his favourite subjects. They were not able to speak Inuit with him.

In 1901, Wallace resigned from the museum amidst allegations of financial scandal. Morris Jesup, President of the museum, withdrew all patronage from Wallace and, therefore, Minik.

In 1904 Rhetta Wallace died

In 1906 Minik discovered through his school friends a horrifying truth: his father's bones were on display in the museum and had been for many years. The Inuit burial of his father's body had been a trick.

In 1907 the New York newspapers took up Minik's story. By this time, William Wallace was impoverished and he and Minik were now living in the inner city of New York.

Minik's case was presented by a New York reporter, Chester Beecroft. Beecroft, Wallace and Minik considered it to be important that:

i) Minik should return to Greenland and

ii) that he should go with an education that would be of use to his fellow Inuits.

Beecroft applied, in vain, to the White House for financial assistance towards Minik's education. Wallace also wrote to Jesup and Peary who continued to ignore Minik's plight.

For the rest of his life, Minik continued to petition the museum for the return of his father's body, but he met with no success. Eventually, Minik left Wallace and went to live with Chester Beecroft, at the age of 18.

By 1909, Minik was keen to return to Greenland, and began to study navigational skills, but pneumonia and depression soon terminated his college career and he ran away. After six weeks Chester Beecroft finally caught up with him in Canada where he had been trying to work his way north, in an attempt to reach Greenland. Minik was very ill and suicidal. Beecroft took him back to New York.

By July 1909, Minik and Beecroft, through their contacts with the newspapers, were succeeding in telling the truth about Peary and damaging his reputation to such an extent that Peary's supporters came to an agreement with them on a plan to help Minik get back to Greenland. Minik arrived in North Star Bay, Greenland, in August 1909. However, he spoke no Inuit and he was a long way south of Etah.

Minik was taken in by one of his relatives, Soqqaq, who helped him re-learn the language and the ways of the Inuit. Minik quickly became a proficient hunter.

In 1910 Minik married an Inuit woman, Arnanaguaq, but they were not happy together and they parted. Although Minik was now healthier than he had been for years, he was never really at ease in Greenland, having been away for so long. In 1913 a new party of American explorers arrived in Etah. Minik was taken on as interpreter and hunter.

In 1916, Minik gained passage on a ship returning to America from Greenland. Having decided to settle in America, he applied for citizenship in 1917 and went to work in a lumbercamp in Pittsburgh, New Hampshire. Minik again contracted pneumonia, this time after a flu epidemic, which swept through the lumbercamps.

He died on the 29th October 1918, aged 29, and was buried in Pittsburgh.

Activities to deepen the children's sense of empathy with Minik

Using a map, or a globe, work out the distance from Minik's home village to New York and then guess the approximate length of time the journey would have taken.

— It is about 2 500 miles as the crow flies, and 3 000 miles by sea. It is as far as London to West Africa.

Key questions

What would the journey have been like for an eight-year-old boy?

Have any of the children experienced long, uncertain journeys?

How would Minik feel surrounded by strangers who speak different languages and have different customs?

Teacher in role

The class is presented with the following information:

MINIK PEARY WALLACE

1890 – 1919

Died from pneumonia in a lumbercamp in Pittsburgh, New Hampshire

Aged 29 years

The teacher explains that he will go into role as Chester Beecroft, Minik's best friend, imagining that he has just found the grave of his friend in a lumbercamp, after searching for him for several years.

The children's role is to find out as much as they can about the friendship and the significant events of Minik's life. The following pointers may help teachers to visualise the potential of the story, but it is difficult to give specific instruction:

◆   Minik has been given the name of Peary, the explorer who brought him to be placed in the Museum when he was eight years old;

◆   In one day alone, 20 000 people came to see Minik and his family arrive in New York, on Peary's ship the *SS Hope*;

◆   The Inuits were placed in a basement flat to be studied;

- Minik had to learn American and forget his Inuit 'way of life' once he was adopted by the Wallaces;

- Minik could never settle in either Greenland or America.

The hot-seating of Chester Beecroft can be as long and as detailed as the teacher feels is appropriate. The teacher will need to have prepared the role, by reading the full story but not be afraid to come out of role when questions are asked which are difficult to answer.

Still images

Ask the children to imagine that the Museum decided to commission a set of oil paintings about the bringing of Minik from Greenland to the Museum. The paintings were given the following titles:

1. Striking the Bargain! (Between Peary and Minik's father.)

2. The voyage on the SS *Hope*.

3. 20 000 People!

4. Life in the Museum basement.

These still images will have the potential for a detailed exploration of some key questions:

— how is history presented?

— how should we present images of Greenland knowing what we now know?

The images can be examined by the teacher making use of many of the strategies described in the Guide (page 43), such as Speaking Thoughts, Living Pictures, Modelling, etc.

After a suitable period of time, it may be worth comparing this drama work, in terms of values and attitudes, to the first mimed film activities on 'The life of the Eskimo'.

Using maps, photographs and records

After the children have located the Arctic Ocean, Canada, New York City, St Lawrence River, the North Pole and Arctic Ocean on the map, provide them with some photographs of New England and Greenland to develop their skills at interpreting visual evidence and contextualising Minik's story more accurately.

Research the contrasting temperatures in New York and Greenland and compare their seasonal changes.

An information sheet

The Inuit people

The first Inuit came from Asia to Alaska 8 000 years ago.

An Englishman, Martin Frobisher, led the first expedition to search for the North West passage and in 1576 became the first Englishman to have met an Inuit.

Early encounters between Inuit and Europeans often ended in tragedy, Inuits were killed or captured and brought back to Europe where they were put on exhibition; most died.

By the seventeenth century fur was increasingly in demand. But it was the whalers that had the greatest impact on the Inuit. Each year hundreds of boats set sail in search of the whale to provide oil, baleen, and whalebone. They wiped out the sea mammals and often other wildlife that the Inuit depended on.

At the same time, the Inuit depended on the whalers for trade and jobs. When the whaling industry collapsed in 1912 the massacre of wildlife made it difficult for the Inuit to return to their old way of life.

The Inuit Language

The Inuit language had over seventy words for snow, but there was not a single word for war.

In schools established by missionaries, the children were not allowed to speak the Inuit language.

GLOSSARY

ESKIMO	A word meaning 'eaters of raw flesh'.
IGLOOS	Inuit shelters made from blocks of snow, used by hunters, now generally defunct.
INUIT	A word meaning 'The People'. (This is the word by which the Inuit like to be known).
INUK	One Inuit person
KAYAK	The Inuit sealskin-covered boat.
KOMATIKS	Inuit dog-sleds.
KUDLIKS	Lamps which were used for lighting and cooking. They burned whale or seal oil.

1 Talk

About any zoos which the children have visited or seen on television.

What animals did they see?

What did they like best?

Was there anything that they didn't like about the zoo?

2 Mime

Introduce the imaginary Beresford Zoo.

Working in groups, children represent visitors to the Zoo. They should decide on what the group is doing: looking at an animal, riding on the Zoo Train, queuing for tickets, having a picnic etc.

The task is to show the rest of the class what is happening, without having children pretending to be animals. Can we tell what they are looking at, or doing by their position or movements? Perhaps they are looking up at a giraffe or moving their heads as they watch a monkey swing.

3 Enactment

Beresford Zoo is in trouble.

The lions need a new cage: the old one is far too small and might become unsafe if the iron rusts any more.

The monkeys have had babies and we want to keep them all together, but that means a bigger cage too.

The cafe has had to be closed because the roof leaks.

Not enough people are coming to the zoo and the owners want a new star attraction - a Giant Panda. However, there is no cage for it: one would have to be built.

There is enough money to do only one of these jobs. As a class discuss all the options in role as the people who run the zoo.

What should be done?

Make the facilities better for the visitors, so that they will bring in more money?

Bring in new animals?

Take more care of the animals you already have?

Split into groups, give a time limit, and ask the groups to each come up with a plan for helping the zoo.

Then hear and discuss each plan.

Snapshot Key Stage 2
(seven to nines)
Zoos

Learning focus

What are zoos for?

How should we care for animals in zoos?

5 Drawing and talk

In groups, children design Beresford Zoo as they would like it to be in ten year's time.

What animals will there be, in what types of enclosure?

Will the zoo keep wild animals at all, or will it be more like a theme park using models and computer images of animals?

How will the zoo attract more visitors?

End with groups sharing their ideas with the rest of the class and answering questions about their plans.

4 Small Group Playmaking

A television company has used the zoo for some filming, and in return they offer a free television advert on their station.

Groups make up their own advertisements.

First talk about what will go in the advert:

Will it focus on the fun to be had on a visit to the zoo?

Will it show how the zoo is trying to care for its animals?

Will it feature the plans to bring over a Giant Panda?

Stress the importance of an advert getting over its message in a short space of time with clear words and actions, perhaps finishing with a catchy slogan.

1 Dramatic playing

Ask the children to imagine how the people felt at the beginning of the story before Giant became unhappy. Working in groups of three or four, ask them to act out their typical day on the mountain. Prompts might include picnics, hide and seek, fishing or flower picking. If it is necessary to focus the dramatic playing, perhaps ask the children to demonstrate one way in which their activities damaged the mountain.

2 Sound pictures

Working in family groups of three or four, make a collage of the sounds and voices which might have been heard when everyone realised that Giant had left. Ideas might include early morning sounds, voices calling from windows, children hurrying to the empty space, the sounds of Giant's feet or voices of people falling off the mountain.

3 Building a new 'Giant'

Using scrap paper, chairs, tables and anything else that might be available, construct the new mountain in the centre of the drama space. Each child can bring one item and place it in the centre of the room, with careful guidance.

i) Ask the children to meet in family groups of three or four, all around the new 'Giant', discussing their feelings about the new creation. Do they have any regrets? Will it serve the same purpose?

ii) Ask the children to represent the adults in the community, standing in a whole class still picture to show their attitudes to the new 'Giant'.

iii) Ask the children to represent the children in the community, showing their attitudes to the new 'Giant'. What do we know about the children's and the adults' views as a result of our still pictures?

Snapshot Key Stage 2
Seven to nines

Giant

Giant by Juliet and Charles Snape (Walker Books) appeals to a wide range of ages, from top infants to lower juniors.

Giant is a mountain. She provides the local community with a place to play and to work. One night, having grown weary of being misused by the community, she leaves, and the people try to construct their own mountain from waste materials. Eventually Lia, a young girl, finds Giant and asks her to return. Giant has been lonely without the community and agrees.

The children should be read the story before beginning any of the activities.

7 Whole-group drama

A meeting of the local community has been called in order to discuss what should be done now that Giant has left. Teacher is in role as the person chairing the meeting, children as members of the community.

6 Still pictures

What will the community look like in ten years' time? Images in small and whole groups.

What would a painting of these events include?

Make a whole-class, still image of the new 'Giant'.

Make two small-group still pictures of people's reactions in the local shop:

i) when the people hear of Giant's leaving

ii) when the people hear she has returned.

Discuss the different reactions within the two images.

5 Teacher roles for hot-seating

- A leader of the community seeking advice from the people now that Giant has left. What is to be done?

- Lia being questioned by the community when she tells them she has found Giant at the seashore.

- A child from another village who had been watching the strange events.

- A farmer whose living is ruined by the new 'Giant', with all its household waste (ie the sheep have nowhere to graze, crops will not grow...).

4 Pair work

i) What does Lia say to her mother about Giant's disappearance?

Try it out then change roles and talk about Lia's feelings. Discuss the different feelings with the whole class.

ii) Does Giant say anything more to Lia than what the story tells us? In pairs, try out what you think might have been said at the seashore.

iii) One person is Giant moving to the sea, the other is a villager, watching. Present a short mime sequence showing what happened.

1 Enactment - Finding the fossils

If your class is familiar with a few dinosaur species, they can use a fossil hunt as the way into this work.

You will need a clear space and large sheets of paper.

Prepare the space by drawing the outlines of dinosaur remains on the paper. Cut these out and then cut up each shape to create a simple jigsaw with three, four or five pieces. Place these around the space under other sheets or P.E. mats, ensuring that the dinosaurs are split up.

When the class enters the space, explain that they are in Mexico to work as palaeontologists - dinosaur researchers. They will work in teams, and each team has an area of the space to explore.

When they remove a covering, they must first look at all the remains and how they are lying together. They might then sketch what they see.

They should carefully remove the remains one by one, trying to identify the dinosaur by the shape of the fragment that they have.

Finally bring all the groups together and, working as a class, piece together the different dinosaurs, using everyone's fragments to make whole fossils.

NOTE: this whole exercise needs the focus of role to stop it becoming an unfocused game. Keep stressing the need for careful, co-ordinated work.

2 Enactment - Discussing the fossils

Still in role as palaeontologists, discuss what you have found, giving an opportunity for children to use their knowledge about dinosaurs. As a class, move around from shape to shape, naming it and sharing any information individuals have about it.

Snapshot Key Stage 2
(seven to nines)
Dinosaurs

Learning focus

Using the evergreen topic of dinosaurs to focus on ownership of historic remains.

3 Discussion and letter writing

Explain that it is now time to take the fossil bones back to Britain, but that when you come to pack them up, you receive a letter from the Mexican Government. Ask a child to read the letter overleaf out to everyone.

Discuss the class' response to the letter. Do they agree, or should the British be allowed to take some remains home as the discoverers of the site?

Split into groups to write a letter in response. Share the letters with the whole class and discuss how you think the authorities will respond in each case.

4 Still Pictures and headlines

In the same groups, children prepare a newspaper photograph and headline on the day that the palaeontologists return to Britain. The picture should attempt to convey the thoughts and feelings of those involved, as well as what actually happened.

Government House
Mexico City

Dear British Palaeontologists,

We thank you for your excellent work in our country,
we could never have uncovered so many valuable remains
without the help of your expert team.

I am sorry to have to inform you that it will not be
possible for you to take the fossils out of the
country. We are going to build a museum on the site
and display the bones there.

Thank you again for your fine work.

Yours sincerely,

Chief Research Scientist

Key Stage 2

Nine- to eleven-year-olds

Return to Earth

Learning focus

Ecology - the Earth and its resources. Our relationship to the planet.

Curriculum links

- The Earth in space
- Climate and weather
- Citizenship

Context

This section is based on a unit of the BBC School Radio series *Drama Workshop*. It has proved popular with the target age range, promoting considerable response on each transmission. A synopsis is given below.

Synopsis

The drama is set at a time in the future when the Earth has been evacuated and the entire population moved to orbiting cities while the planet's climate and ecology is transformed to make it ideal for human habitation. This process is known as Ecoforming.

The class role is that of residents of Station 4, one of the orbiting cities. They have won a visit to the Earth to see Ecoforming in action. Once there, the class has the opportunity to sabotage the process, returning the Earth to a more 'natural' state with (as the authorities would see it) unpredictable weather, unreliable food production, the possibility of earthquakes, tornados and floods. The drama pivots on this crucial moment of decision which involves weighing questions of our relationship to the global environment, our rights to interfere for what some see as a good ultimate purpose, and the issue of acting illegally for what may seem a greater good.

With its imaginative, science fiction background, the material seeks to open up these difficult questions in an exciting and engaging manner.

How to use the material

There is a lot of material here! We have used a sequential structure developed from the School Radio programmes. This is certainly not the only way of dealing with these issues. It is simply the structure used in the programmes and presents an example of the development of an idea through various drama strategies.

The material would spread over several drama sessions, or could be used occasionally within other work on the theme. You might choose, for example, to set up the life of Station 4 using written work and CDT, moving into the drama activity The Ecoformer (see below).

As ever in drama, work can expand and contract to fit your children's and your own way of working.

Drama forms

Moving into the future

Aim: to begin work on the material by engaging interest in Station 4 and its way of life.

Getting started on a new topic is always difficult. It involves engaging interest and stimulating involvement, whilst giving the necessary background information. Try to get into the practical activity as quickly as possible.

Explain that we are going to work in drama by imagining a time in the future when everybody lives in large space cities in Earth orbit.

Introduce the term 'Ecoforming' (the changing and control of a planet's climate and environment).

Talk to the children about their role as school pupils on Station 4.

As a class, discuss what might be different about schooling in such a situation as compared with now.

Ask the children to work in groups to produce a Still Picture showing one aspect of school life on Station 4.

Take time to look at each picture and then allow the groups to explain what is happening in each case. Use this to begin building shared ideas about life on Station 4.

Teaching points

What is our life like on Station 4? Can you sum it up in just one word or a couple of words?

What are the good points about life on Station 4? What are the bad points?

Class meeting

Aim: to add depth to the picture of life on Station 4, particularly in relation to the authoritarian nature of the City Elders.

As a class, the children formally enter the Space Station Meeting Hall.

Choose an area of your teaching space to represent the Meeting Hall and decide where the entrance is to be. Start the drama with everyone outside the entrance and then work out a way of coming in which is respectful, formal, slightly solemn - as if entering a court, or processing in a church service. This could involve entering in small groups, or in two lines - adopting preset standing positions and waiting in absolute silence.

Devise a salute together as a class and use it every time there is a need of formality.

When everything is ready, the Elders enter and ask everyone to sit. The Elders are the Teacher in Role and two or three class members. If you feel that class members are not yet ready to take on such a distinctive role, you can undertake this yourself.

Before starting the drama, be clear with the elders that they have a simple message to impart.

The Elders are pleased with the class' work. They have won the annual prize of a trip to Earth to see humanity's greatest achievement -Ecoforming in action. They will leave tomorrow and return in one month's time. Are there any questions?

The heart of the drama is in the questions asked and the Elders' responses. It may well be necessary to move out of the situation to discuss this.

What sort of questions might you ask? Will everyone be happy about a trip to Earth at such short notice? What if our parents don't want us to go? Does anyone feel unhappy about the whole idea of Ecoforming?

Use this discussion to set up questions, some of which can allow the Elders to demonstrate their authoritarian approach when you re-enter the drama situation.

There is no choice in this situation. It is your duty to go. Your parents will be informed.

When you do re-run, you might decide to go right back to the formal entry in order to re-establish the mood of the meeting.

> **NOTE**
>
> It may be that your class will react strongly to the tone of the Elders, maybe even suggesting strikes or rebellion in response. Here you will face a choice which is typical of drama situations - to what extent do you go with the children's responses, possibly taking the drama off in a totally new direction? The answer to this will depend on a number of factors

— the conviction and depth of the children's response

— your judgement on the sustainability of the new direction

— your judgement of your own ability to use appropriate drama forms to meet the new direction.

This could be an exciting opportunity to develop a new drama story about Station 4, but if you feel unhappy with this direction you should share your doubts with the class, challenging the reality of, for example, a strike in such an ordered community.

Teaching points

What do you think about the fact that you have to go?

Think of some descriptive words that would fit the Elders.

The journey

Aim: to employ Small Group Playmaking to depict a journey through space and the feelings which accompany it.

There are a number of ways that the space journey can be enacted. A possible structure is suggested here, but you might also like to consider:

♦ Group poetry writing/performing

♦ Movement - Dance/drama

♦ Painting and models.

To depict the journey as part of continuing drama work, explain that the children are going to work in groups to prepare a presentation showing the journey.

Start as a whole class, preparing lists of words related to the space journey.

Split these into Describing Words and Feeling Words.

Have the list written down where it is available to all the groups as they work, then set each group the task of choosing a key moment from the journey which they can present in a Still Picture, and to choose words to speak out loud, individually as they hold their picture. Each set of words are to include describing and feeling words.

Example

A group may show the final moment of parting from family and friends as the children are strapped into their seats.

As they hold the pictures, each group member speaks a word or thought:

> 'I don't want to go now.'
> 'I wish we could get on with it.'
> 'I'm scared.'
> 'Alone!'

This could be developed by the groups moving into a second picture (as the hatch is closed for example), speaking further thoughts which fit the new situation.

See each group's work and, if time allows, let the class suggest refinements. Alternatively run all the groups at the same time with you orchestrating who speaks when.

Teaching points

Why did each group choose those particular moments. What was it that made them feel special?

How will people of the future view space journeys? Will they seem as ordinary as a car journey now?

The Ecoformer

Aim: to explore the nature of Ecoforming.

The first task in this session is to create a class consensus on what an Ecoformer is and what it does.

Explain that the children have been taken to an Ecoformer site - a large factory, completely automatic with some robots. Its purpose is to monitor the Earth's weather, volcanoes and earthquakes, and make changes to form an ideal world.

Initiate out-of-role discussion on what changes would need to be made to the Earth to make it more hospitable for humans.

Value and record ideas as they are suggested, but keep pushing the discussion forward by asking probing questions:

'Would dangerous animals be eliminated?'

'Tigers can harm people - though not very often, should we cage them? Kill them? Change their nature by genetic engineering?'

'What about the natural enemies of our food - crop infesting beetles for example? Flies and other insects that carry disease - would they all be eliminated?'

'Would we destroy forests to make more room for people to live? If we did, what would happen to the creatures which live there?'

A major aim of the discussion is to give the children enough material with which to create 'Video Films' for the Ecoformer Visitors' Centre. They do this by working in Small Group Playmaking. The 'Video' (which could really be recorded if you have the equipment and time) is to explain the aim and nature of Ecoforming from the point of view of its supporters.

For example, children could present a simple Before and After advert for ecoforming using two still or living pictures with a commentary. The Before picture and commentary paint a picture of a dangerous, unpredictable world - the After suggests a perfect environment for humans.

Teaching points

What makes the videos good advertisements for Ecoforming?

Decision

Aim: to decide whether or not to destroy the Ecoformer.

Discuss the children's own views of Ecoforming, giving an opportunity for expression of the resentment that will have built up.

Again, be prepared to ask provocative questions to generate discussion if necessary.

- Is the earth ours to do with as we wish?

- Do animals have rights?

- Isn't it better to have an unpredictable environment - wouldn't it be boring if everything were perfect?

Set up the following situation:

It is evening on the Earth, everyone is enjoying the open skies and freshness of a real world. In their groups the children are sitting together around a campfire, talking about their experiences.

Ask them to hold a secret meeting to decide what to do about the Ecoformer. Let one person in each group tentatively suggest that they should destroy it and see how the others react - can they make up a plan?

Point out that there are other people around, adults from the Space Station, so ideas must be discussed quietly, and with an eye to who is near by.

You could walk around between the groups, acting as a guard - the groups must not let you hear anything suspicious.

When the groups are close to a moment of decision, employ a simple ritual. The class stands in a circle around the fire. Let each person consider carefully if they intend to join in the destruction of the Ecoformer. Then, on your signal, those in favour could:

— step forward - those against, step back;

— place their identity badges in a pile;

or you could simply go round the circle and let each person state their intentions.

Options

The destruction of the Ecoformer is difficult to enact with any sense of realism. It needs strong control factors to prevent a breakdown in the tension and reality of the situation. It may be better to go straight on to the next section where the consequences of the action are examined.

On the other hand, children may feel cheated if they do not find some way of marking this event. You could use:

— Still Pictures - a set of three pictures showing key moments and the tension of being discovered.

— Movement - a slow motion sequence using music to give atmosphere and tension.

— A game-type activity where the group enacts the disconnecting of various pieces of equipment in silence while you move about the space. If you see anyone move they are detected by a robot and must leave with their task unfinished.

— A collective Narration where each child tells part of the story of the destruction.

What are the good and bad points about interfering with the Ecoformer?

Does this feel like a difficult decision? Why?

Shouldn't we just obey the elders who sent us on the trip and talk through our grievances with them?

Trial

Aim: to provide a role situation where all the issues raised within the drama can be considered.

Whatever decisions were reached by individuals, the implications of this and the whole situation of the drama can be explored in a trial.

Back on Station 4, the Elders are concerned that the school trip has gone so wrong. They want to know what happened and why, they cannot understand how anyone could object to the Ecoforming of the planet.

Set up the trial with a small group of those who voted to destroy the Ecoformer as the accused, yourself and some of the children as Elders, some as the jury and others as witnesses who can be called upon to recall everything that happened in the drama.

The situation should not be based solely on present court proceedings. You could allow anyone to ask questions - with the Elders' permission, but as in the first activity, try to keep the atmosphere formal.

Teaching points

End with a class discussion and vote on the actions of those who sought to destroy the equipment.

Were they vandals?

Were they acting in the interests of the planet?

The Gunpowder Plot

The prospect of exploring historical contexts through drama is an exciting one: seemingly distant or remote events can be made more immediate and children are able to question the motives and relationships of those involved, as well as the manner in which the stories have been interpreted.

Learning focus

— To enable the children to recognise that the Gunpowder Plot was a consequence of religious differences.

— To recognise the connections between modern Bonfire Night celebrations and the original Gunpowder Plot.

— To appreciate the significance of recounting historical events from a particular perspective.

Curriculum links

History
R.E.

Context

The story of the Gunpowder Plot is one which has been told and re-told to generations of children. Yet there still remains a suprising lack of general understanding about the connection between the throwing of a 'Guy' on the bonfire each November 5th, and the events at the Houses of Parliament in 1605.

The following description of practical ideas draws together some of the issues from our planning framework and suggests a way in which The Gunpowder Plot might be introduced to children through drama.

Although each of the structures can be used as a self-contained entity, they would be effective as a progressive sequence of activities in a longer session. It is intended that each of the structures can be used in either the classroom or the hall.

Drama forms

Still Pictures (as a whole class)

Aim: to stimulate general thinking about Guy Fawkes and to focus the children's existing knowledge in a collective way.

The children make a full circle, facing outwards, backs to the centre, and the teacher explains that she is going to say some key words and phrases which the children will interpret by creating the first image that comes into their head. On the count of three, the children turn inwards and make the image:

NOVEMBER 5TH   LIGHT THE BONFIRE

FIREWORKS   BONFIRE NIGHT ACCIDENTS!

ROCKET   THE GUY'S ALIGHT!

PENNY FOR THE GUY   THE BONFIRE'S OUT

BANGER

As each image is created, it is usually sufficient to give the children just a few moments to let their eyes go round the circle to see what everyone has created. However, you may feel you want to spend more time considering the images, perhaps by half the class looking at the other's and vice versa.

A brief discussion of the range of feelings and moods the images make is essential at this stage.

The class now goes back to the circle and you explain that this is the final image of this part of the lesson. The key words this time are:

GUY FAWKES

This time the children are encouraged to look closely at the images and to comment on them in some detail.

Brainstorming

Aim: to focus on Guy Fawkes by providing the opportunity for the children to share information in small groups.

Each group of four or five has a large sheet of paper and a felt-tipped pen. On the paper the teacher has put the following questions and drawn a figure:

What do you know about him?

What do you think you know about him?

Anything else?

The children then begin to jot down words, dates, phrases and such like on either side of the figure. Anything that doesn't fit, but which the children feel is important, can be placed at the bottom of the figure.

The ideas are then shared, the class moving from group to group, looking at what has been written or drawn, with appropriate discussion.

The children return to their original groups and are asked to create a still picture which contains two images of Guy Fawkes at the same time. The two images are:

1. Guy Fawkes as he is depicted each year.
2. Guy Fawkes, based on what we think he did on 5 November 1605.

Each of the images is considered and debated. There are suggestions and ideas described in 'Guide to drama forms' on how these group images might be extended and questioned further.

Modelling

Aim: to prompt a consideration of how personal interpretations of historical events influence us.

Before beginning this structure, you will need to decide how much factual information your class will need in order to become involved. This will have been evident during the previous activity. The class is given a copy of the famous engraving 'The Great Conspiracy' (opposite), and asked to discuss it. The following questions are offered as suggestions for the kind of issues the children might begin to get interested in:

How has the painter created a sense of conspiracy?

Why do you think one figure does not have a hat?

Do you think this was painted by someone in favour of the conspiracy, against it, or simply telling the story as it was?

What do you notice about the names?

What kind of relationships do you see in the painting?

What kinds of action do you see in the painting?

You can now choose to ask the children to work in small groups, or as a whole class, explaining the technique(s) of modelling to them.

Modelling is a process of creating and recreating images in Still Picture form in order to develop the meaning and children's understanding. One child can be given sole responsiblity for modelling, or it may be allocated to a group of children. This is a particularly useful strategy when children are engaged in interpreting published photographs or paintings, as in this case.

One of the interesting figures in the painting is that of Bates, who has only one name, no beard, no hat, and who is being given a message. Bates was the man who delivered the gunpowder and who worked for Robert Catesby.

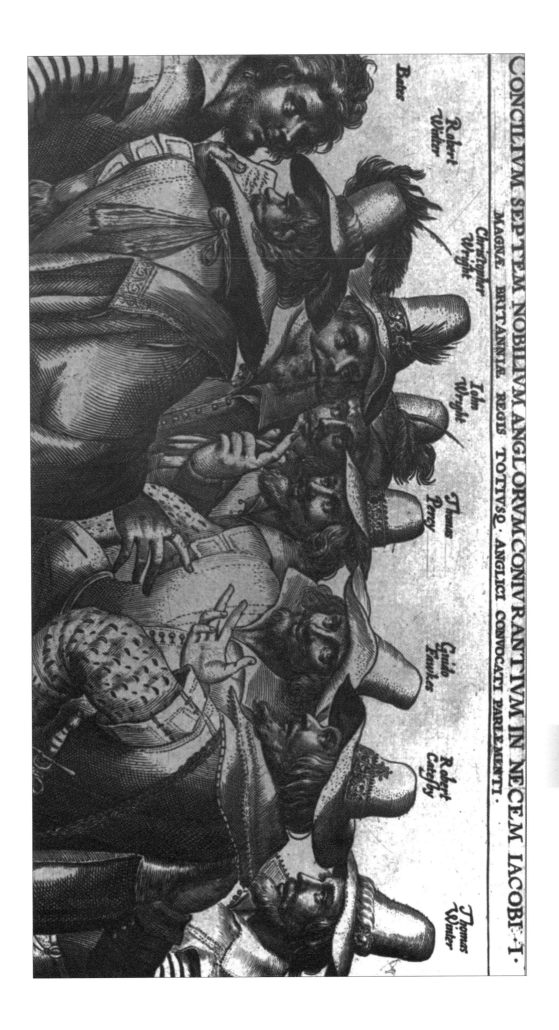

CONCILIVM SEPTEM NOBILIVM ANGLORVM CONIVRANTIVM IN NECEM IACOBI·I·

MAGNÆ BRITANNIÆ REGIS TOTIVSQ̇· ANGLICI CONVOCATI PARLEMENTI·

Bates

Robert
Winter

Christopher
Wright

Iohn
Wright

Thomas
Percy

Guido
Fawkes

Robert
Catesby

Thomas
Winter

Some key tasks

— Model how this painting might look as if you are a painter sympathetic to the plotters' cause.

— Re-model the figures to highlight the plight of Bates.

— Re-model the figures to reflect a secret message which indicates to observers that the painter is actually a sympathiser, despite external appearances.

— Model how the figures would look, with Guy Fawkes represented, as if you are:

     i. making an advert for fireworks today
     ii. making figures for a children's museum

Teacher-in-role

Aim:

To highlight the dilemma of divided loyalty between church and government, which many of the family members and Catholic supporters might have experienced at the time.

The teacher takes on the role of Bates' son, explaining that the role has been made up for the purposes of the drama. The children are asked to take on the roles of the children of the workers on the Catesby estate, who have been called to a secret meeting at which Bates' son explains to them all the events of the plot, his father's role, and subsequent arrests, and the fact that the King's soldiers are coming to search the estate and may question them about him.

He asks them how he should protect himself and seeks their help.

In their role as children of the estate workers, the class will have to face the dilemma of upholding the law of the land or helping a friend.

1 Still Pictures

Instant responses in groups to the keyword: **Pirate.**

Discuss: Were pirates real? What do we know about them? Write down collected knowledge.

2 Living/Still Pictures with narration

In the same groups prepare a drama report for the rest of the class, showing the groups shared knowledge about pirates. For example, three or four Still or Living Pictures linked by 'captions' or narration.

Snapshot Key Stage 2 (nine to twelves)

Pirates

Learning focus

Pirates are not myths

Who were pirates: male/female?

Adventurers? Terrorists?

5 Forum Theatre

Using the results of Small Group Playmaking as a starting point, examine the moment of decision. What choices were really open to the people involved?

With the whole class in role as a ship's crew, some pirates have failed in their attempt to steal gold from your ship. Now you must decide what to do with them - deal with them yourselves, take them prisoner and hand them over to justice, or listen to their suggestion that you join forces?

Let a few take the role of the pirates who claim that the gold was stolen from their country in the first place. Deepen the drama with Still Pictures (telling the Pirates's Story), Speaking Thoughts and Teacher in Role.

4 Small Group Playmaking

Show the moment of decision when one or more people decide to become pirates. Think about a realistic situation, then act it out.

3 Teacher-in-role

Adopt the role of a reluctant pirate, and, by class questioning, reveal why you have become a pirate.

I became a pirate because....

I am a woman whose husband has left me, making me poor.

I wanted adventure and change so when I was offered the chance to join the crew of the White Shark, I took it.

I was falsely accused of a crime, so on my way to be tried, I escaped. Now I have to remain on the wrong side of the law.

I want to make my fortune.

A friend persuaded me that there were riches to be had.

It sort of happened by accident, I just drifted into it.

The Events At Eyam in Derbyshire

Eyam was an isolated village of some 350 inhabitants. In addition to the familiar employment tasks of a seventeenth century village, there were extensive tin mines in the nearby hills.

Following the Restoration of the Monarchy in 1660, the 'old order' was returning and, as part of that process a new Rector was appointed. Eyam was William Mompesson's first living. He replaced the nonconformist Rector of the Commonwealth, Thomas Stanley, who continued to live in the village.

In 1665, the plague in London was at its worst and in September of that year, the Eyam village tailor, George Vickers, received a collection of clothes from his London supplier. Within a week he was dead. By the end of the month five more villagers had died, and twenty-three deaths occurred in October. In just over a year 260 villagers had died of the plague.

William Mompesson, fully aware of all the dangers, persuaded the villagers to isolate themselves, in order to prevent the infection from spreading further. Provisions were brought to the village boundary for collection, in exchange for money. The church was closed and the services and village meetings took place outdoors.

Although they chose to send their own children away, Catherine and William Mompesson remained with the village throughout. In August 1666, Catherine herself caught the disease and died.

Snapshot Key Stage 2
Nine to twelves
Eyam

Learning focus

• to consider the human motives which caused a village to isolate itself

• to examine how the Mompessons could send their children to safety, but ask others to die

• to experience the inter-dependence of families in a small rural village

1. Scene Building

In small groups, using chairs, apparatus, and materials, create the inside of a cottage in Eyam. Who lives there? What work do they do? What is their attitude to Church?

2. Family Signs

Make a sign, out of card, which indicates the character and trade of your family and which is placed outside the cottage.

3. Still Picture

(i) In groups create a picture of a time of celebration for the family, for example harvest, birth marriage. (ii) Create a second image which depicts the family at the end of the year of plague. Create the two pictures one after the other.

4. Hot-Seating

Teacher goes into role as a carter who travelled the area. The children, as themselves, ask the carter questions about what he knew of Eyam, before and after the plague.

5. Teacher-in-role

Create the scene in the market square where Mompesson (teacher-in-role) tells the village (whole class) that he thinks that the plague is in the village. How will they respond?

6. Living Pictures

Bring each of the cottages to life immediately after the meeting in 5. Everyone listens to the conversations taking place about the new Rector and George Vickers, the tailor.

7. Forum Theatre

Create the scene in the Rectory when the Mompessons are trying to decide whether or not to send their children away. Are they right to do this? What did other villagers think?

8. Movement

A movement sequence which illustrates life in the village at the height of the plague. The class mimes all the actions of trying to cope with human tragedy. Music: Lark Ascending by Vaughn Williams.

Appendix A

Games

Many teachers use games as part of their drama work, to fulfil a number of different functions. We recognise the place and value of games within the curriculum, but we do not see them as essential to the drama process. The subject warrants a book of its own and only a small part would concern games in drama. Below, we give a short selection which teachers have found useful.

Games which encourage speaking and listening

Pass the story

A group sits in a circle and one person begins a story, then passes to the next and so on round the circle.

Variations include:

- allowing only one word each

- starting sentences alternately 'Fortunately...' and 'Unfortunately...'

- giving a 'set' story to re-tell.

Speaking Gourd

The 'Gourd' is any object which can be passed from one person to the next as the children sit in a circle - a small stone, pine cone, ruler or whatever. The rule is that an individual may only speak when holding the gourd. A child who wishes to make a contribution to a discussion or story-telling must indicate that she wants the gourd or wait for it to be passed to her.

This can be effective in and out of role.

Games which evoke a sense of tension

Secret messages

Children sit in pairs, facing one another. Two or four children are chosen to be 'guards' and they patrol the space. The aim for the pairs is to pass a secret message - a question from one partner, the answer from the other. If the guards see anyone talking, that pair must sit at the side of the space. The teacher calls a halt after a short time and asks who managed to pass their message successfully. A variation is to require the class to sit in two circles with one partner on the inner circle and the other on the outer.

Wink murder

The class stands in a circle, except for the 'detective' who must leave the room while a 'murderer' is chosen. The detective then returns to stand in the middle of the circle. The murderer begins to wink at victims who must fall to the floor. The detective has three chances to guess the murderer.

Affirming games

One good thing about...

In a circle, each child takes it in turns to say 'One good thing about...' the person on their left.

Labels

Each child writes their name on four slips of paper. All these labels are then put into a bag and each child in the class takes four at random. On each of these four labels, they write a positive thought about the named child.

The slips are remixed so that no-one knows who wrote what, and are distributed so that each child gets back their four labels, now with comments written on them. They can then draw or paint a self portrait to which the labels are attached.

Trust games

Imaginary journey

In pairs, one partner closes his or her eyes. The other gently takes the unseeing partner by the hand and steers them on a journey around the space. Once they have their partner's confidence and have managed to avoid crashes, the journey can take on an imaginative aspect as the seeing partner describes where they might be:

'We're crossing a field, now we must crawl through thick bushes...' and so on.

Circle support

In small groups, one group member stands in the middle of a tight circle. The others put up their hands and support the one in the middle until he or she feels confident enough to 'let go' allowing the group to take their weight and gently move them around the circle. The one in the middle keeps his or her feet still but the top half of their body is moved entirely by the rest of the group.

Appendix B

Primary Drama Record

NAME						
AGE	HIGH			LOW		
YEAR	**1**	**2**	**3**	**4**	**5**	**EVIDENCE**
THE ABILITY TO CREATE DRAMA						
◆ TO WORK AND PLAN WITH OTHERS;						
◆ TO ORGANISE AND SHAPE MATERIAL.						
THE ABILITY TO ENGAGE IN DRAMA						
◆ TO USE APPROPRIATE DRAMA OR THEATRE SKILLS;						
◆ TO PARTICIPATE IN DIFFERENT DRAMA CONTEXTS.						
THE ABILITY TO REFLECT ON DRAMA						
◆ TO RECOGNISE QUALITIES IN THE DRAMA AND POSE ALTERNATIVES;						
◆ TO EVALUATE PERSONAL CONTRIBUTION TO THE GROUP.						
CONTEXT OF LESSON						

Teachers comments

Signed ....

Childrens comments

Signed ....

Appendix C

The role of the curriculum consultant

Many schools find it useful to have a curriculum consultant for drama who undertakes the following responsibilities:

- provides the head and governing body with specialist advice concerning the teaching of drama within the school;
- facilitates effective policy-writing which will enable whole-school development in drama;
- informs staff of recent developments in drama teaching methodology;
- oversees the school's resourcing for drama and ensures that these resources are effectively co-ordinated;
- liaises with other schools, primary, special and secondary, to ensure continuity and progression.

Key tasks would be to:

- carry out an initial whole-school audit of drama expertise and resources. Avoid any temptation to make assumptions about staff skills, classroom practice or previous training.
- attend INSET and area meetings of similar consultants, informing staff of any available support.
- make sure that drama is always considered within the school's development planning;
- encourage, support and guide all staff to teach drama with their own classes, but try not to take responsibility for all the teaching;
- offer to speak to the governing body about current developments in your subject area;
- promote parental involvement and understanding of drama, through meetings, workshops or discussion;
- prepare clear guidance and a realistic time-line for the writing of a drama policy. Don't take this task on alone - all staff should take part;
- collect photographs, stories and images which have proved useful, supported by teaching notes and ideas on how they were used;
- maintain a library of BBC radio and television programmes, with the appropriate follow-up notes; develop a collection of props.

Appendix D

*Some critical questions designed to help a
school prepare a drama policy*

General teaching issues

Is drama being taught throughout the school at the moment?
How can drama address equal opportunity issues?
How do we define drama: is it different to play/theatre/games?
Are we all comfortable teaching drama?
Is our drama biased towards process or performance?
What kinds of support do we need to develop and deepen our
drama teaching
- knowledge?
- confidence?
- ideas?
- skills?
- resources?
- suitable times and spaces?
Are we providing adequate opportunities for the children to
develop their learning through the imagined experience?

Curriculum issues

When, where and how should drama feature in our curriculum
planning?
How could we use drama to teach the published cross-
curricular themes?

Assessment

How can we ensure continuity and progression in drama?
Do we need to assess individual or group achievement in
drama?
Do we need to report achievement in drama to parents?

Resources

What kinds of resources are useful for drama?
Do we make good use of professional artists?
How can we ensure that resources are available to the whole
staff?
Are we making the most of the community as a resource?

Appendix E

Bibliography

Classroom practice

2D Indians and Pioneers (Unfinished Materials) 2D Publications.

Games for Actors and Non-Actors A Boal; translated by Adrian Jackson (Routledge 1992).

Practical Primary Drama G Davies (Heinemann 1983).

Making Sense of Classroom Drama J Neelands (Heinemann 1984).

Structuring Drama Work J Neelands (Cambridge University Press 1990).

Drama Guidelines O'Neill and Lambert et al (Heinemann 1976).

Drama Structures O'Neill and Lambert (Hutchinson 1972).

100+ Ideas for Drama A Sher (Heinemann 1975).

The Teaching of Drama In the Primary School B Woolland (Longman 1993).

Theory of drama

Drama in Schools Arts Council (Arts Council Education, 14 Great Peter Street, London SW1P 3NQ; 1992)

Drama as Education G Bolton (Longman 1984).

New Perspectives on Classroom Drama G Bolton (Simon & Schuster 1992).

Towards a Theory of Drama in Education G Bolton (Longman 1979).

Drama 5-16 DES (Curriculum Matters 17; HMSO 1989).

Collected Writings D Heathcote (Hutchinson 1984).

The Teaching and Learning of Drama HMI (Aspects of Primary Education; HMSO 1990).

Dorothy Heathcote: Drama as a Learning Medium BJ Wagner (Hutchinson 1979)

Books on theatre which have influenced classroom practice

The Theatre of the Oppressed A Boal (Theatre Communications Group, 1979).

Exploring Theatre and Education K Robinson (Heinemann 1980).

Theatre-in-education

Learning Through Theatre ed T jackson (Manchester University Press 1980).

Theatre-in-Education J O'Toole (Hodder & Stoughton 1976).

Can Theatre Teach? C Reddington (Pergamon 1983).

Drama and other arts

Living Powers: The Arts in Education P Abbs (Falmer 1987).

The Arts in Schools (Gulbenkian Foundation 1983).

Journal and magazines

Drama (three issues annually)
National Drama Publications
4 Oaklands
Gosforth
Newcastle-upon-Tyne
NE3 4VQ

Standing Conference for Young People's Theatre (SCYPT) *SCYPT Journal*,
The Dukes,
Moor Lane,
Lancaster, LA1 1QE

2D Magazine (two issues annually)
2D Publications
33 Cannock Street
Leicester
LE4 7HR

Appendix F

Radio and television

School radio drama

At the time of writing, BBC School Radio offers three weekly series aimed at supporting curriculum drama:

LET'S MAKE A STORY is aimed at the five-to seven-year-old age-range and is closely focused on speaking and listening.

FIRST STEPS IN DRAMA is for Key Stage 2 children aged seven to nine years. It features units of two or more programmes which explore a range of curriculum areas.

DRAMA WORKSHOP offers a similar style to *First Steps in Drama*, but with an older perspective (nine- to twelve-year-olds) and more complex activities. It is also popular in the lower years of secondary school.

Each series is supported by teacher's notes which give background information and advice on the drama activities in the programmes.

The programmes are designed to be recorded off air, allowing the teacher to pause the tape as appropriate. They offer all the strengths of radio drama: strong performances, evocative music and imaginative sound effects, engaging children in imagining the scenes and characters for themselves as they listen.

A narrator then sets up drama activities for the children to enact. Over a term of programmes the activities will cover the full range of approaches in this book. Many teachers find the series useful in providing a clear structure for their drama work. Others use the material as a starting point, switching off the tape after a particularly powerful or thought-provoking scene, and then developing their own work on the theme.

Used imaginatively, and seen as a resource to be mediated by the teacher, the programmes offer a flexible approach to primary drama.

Details of all BBC Schools programmes can be found in the Annual Programme sent free to all schools and are available BBC Education Information, White City, London W12 7TS.

Other BBC television and radio.

Many television programmes, particularly those broadcast for schools, can be used to initiate drama, to stimulate thought and to provide useful information in, for example, a historical context.

The popular BBC Schools programme *Zig Zag* will often feature historical material which can be explored using the approaches outlined in this book.

English Express, with a focus on written and spoken language, often features drama, poetry and issues which are rich in possibilities for exploration through curriculum drama. The teacher's notes accompanying the series give further support.

Landmarks and *Watch*, known to many primary teachers, can also be used as initial stimuli for drama and can provide factual backup and support. Schools Television Primary Science programmes can also be used in this way.

On School Radio, the Primary Music Course (*Song Tree, Music Workshop and Time and Tune*) often features drama elements geared towards performance. The popular dance programmes, *Let's Move, Time to Move* and *Dance Workshop* can also be useful in developing movement and imaginative skills.